Recipes From Peggy's Cove

Illustrated by pictures of Peggy's Cove

Photograph on front cover — World famous *Bluenose II* passing Peggy's Cove Light. Photograph on back cover — c. 1925.

ISBN 0-88999-364-5
printed by
Lancelot Press Limited
Hantsport, N.S.
1987

Acknowledgements

William E. deGarthe's sculptural tribute to fishermen.

The Peggy's Cove Preservation Society gratefully acknowledges the contribution of the following people in compiling these favourite recipes: Eliza Beale, Fay Beale, Jo Beale, Marjorie Campbell, Gertie Crooks, Marie Crooks, Rita Crooks, Sheila Crooks, Judy Dauphinee, Agnes DeGarthe, Minnie Dunn, Roberta Fralick, Frances Garrison, Alice Lanning, Elizabeth Leadon, Gracie Manuel, Gwyneth Manuel, Denise Morash, Edith Morash, Judy Morash, Norma Morash, Stephen O'Leary, Nellie Seaboyer, George Swinimer, Madelyn Wallace. Also thanks to those people who contributed the photographs for this book.

This cook book is printed by Lancelot Press for the Peggy's Cove Preservation Society. Proceeds from its sale will be used for the society's projects in Peggy's Cove.

Contents

The Peggy's Cove Preservation Society was incorporated on February 4, 1983 for the purpose of providing a representative voice in matters affecting the future of the community.

Soups

Peggy's Cove around 1940

Current view of Peggy's Cove

Fish Chowder *very good*

2 lb. haddock or cod fillets
1/4 lb. salt pork, diced 1/2 inch
1/2 c. finely chopped onion
3 c. thinly sliced potato
2 c. water
5 c. milk
6 oz. evaporated milk (3 x 1/2)
8 soda crackers, finely crushed
3 tbsp. butter
2 tbsp. chopped parsley
1/4 tsp. pepper

Cut fish in bite size pieces. Saute pork until crisp; remove and drain. Add onions to drippings and cook until tender but not brown. Stir in potatoes and water; cover and cook until potatoes are tender (about 10 minutes). Add fish 10 minutes before serving. Cover and simmer. In another pot, heat milk, cracker crumbs, butter, parsley and seasonings. Combine with first mixture and heat until thoroughly blended, but do not boil. Garnish with crisp pork pieces.

8 to 10 servings

Creamed Potato Soup

2 small onions, diced
1/2 c. chopped celery
1/4 lb. or 5 tbsp. butter
2 medium potatoes, cubed
1 1/2 c. chicken stock
1 c. cream
salt and pepper to taste
chopped chives

Cook chopped onions and celery in 2 tbsp. of butter until soft. Wash, peel and cube potatoes and add to onion and celery. Add chicken stock and cook until potatoes are tender. Sieve the mixture. Add cream and 2 tbsp. of butter. Season to taste. Serve hot or chilled with topping of chives.

4 servings

6

Lobster Soup

1/2 lb. lobster meat cut in small pieces
2 tbsp. butter
1/2 c. onion, chopped fine
1/2 c. celery, chopped fine
2 tbsp. flour
2 c. milk
1 c. whipping cream
2 tbsp. dry sherry
1 tsp. lemon juice
1/2 tsp. salt
  cayenne
  parsley

Saute celery and onion in butter for about 5 minutes. Blend in flour and seasonings and cook over low heat. Slowly stir in the milk and cook until smooth and thick. Add lobster and cream, remove from heat; stir in sherry and lemon juice. Sprinkle each portion with a bit of chipped parsley and cayenne.

6 servings

Onion Soup au Poisson

1 lb. fillets, cut in bite size pieces
4 c. sliced onions
4 bouillon cubes, beef or chicken
4 c. boiling water
1 tbsp. margarine, melted
1/2 tsp. salt
1/8 tsp. pepper
  grated parmesan cheese

Cook onion rings in a covered saucepan until tender over low heat. Season with salt and pepper. Dissolve bouillon cubes in boiling water and add to onions. Bring mixture to a boil stirring constantly. Add fish and cook approximately 10 minutes until fish flakes easily. Garnish with cheese.

4 servings

Lobster Bisque

8 oz. lobster chopped fine
1/2 c. cracker crumbs
1 small onion minced
Paprika
2 tbsp. butter
1 qt. milk
salt & pepper

Melt butter in deep saucepan over low heat, stirring constantly. Gradually add milk, cracker crumbs, onion and salt and pepper to taste. Blend thoroughly. When smooth, add lobster. Simmer over low heat for five minutes or until lobster is thoroughly heated. Sprinkle servings with paprika.

Shrimp Bisque

1 lb. zucchini, sliced
2 medium carrots, sliced
1/2 c. celery, chopped
1/2 c. green onion, sliced
1 tbsp. flour
1 3/4 c. milk
2 c. water
1 10 oz. can cream of mushroom soup
1/2 c. sour cream
1/2 c. dry white wine
2 tsp. instant chicken bouillon
8 oz. shrimp

Cook zucchini, carrots, celery and green onion in butter for about 20 minutes till vegetables are tender. Stir in flour, add all milk at once. Cook and stir till thick, continue cooking for a minute longer. Pour in a blender and blend until smooth. Meanwhile in pot, combine water, soup, sour cream, wine and bouillon. Stir in blended mixture and shrimp. Heat thoroughly, do not boil.

6 servings

Pea Soup

2 lb. pork hocks
1/2 lb. mild Italian sausage, cooked and cut in 1/2 inch pieces
1 lb. split peas
2 qt. water
6 leeks, sliced
4 stalks celery, sliced
2 cloves garlic, chopped
1 1/2 tsp. savory leaves, crushed
1 1/2 tsp. salt
1/2 tsp. pepper

Boil peas and water for 2 minutes. Remove from heat and let stand covered for approximately 1 hour. Add all remaining ingredients except sausage and bring to a boil. Reduce heat and simmer about 2 hours (or until pork is tender). Skim fat. Remove pork and cut in 1/2 inch pieces; return to soup with sausages. Heat to boiling, reduce heat and simmer another 15 minutes.

8 servings

Onion Soup

2 large onions
2 tbsp. butter
1 tsp. flour
1 — 10 oz. can consomme
salt and pepper to taste
gruyere or mozzarella cheese
french bread

Peal and slice very thinly onions, separating rings. Heat butter in large saucepan; add onion rings and cook very gently over low heat, stirring almost constantly with a wooden spoon until rings are golden brown. Sprinkle with flour. When this has been well blended, gradually stir in consomme diluted with 1 can of water. Stir constantly until soup begins to boil. Lower heat; cover the pan and simmer for about 20 minutes. Season to taste. To serve: Toast 4 slices of bread. Place a slice in each bowl and pour the soup over it. Sprinkle each bowl with grated cheese. Place bowls in a 400°F oven to melt and brown cheese. Pass extra cheese to sprinkle over the tops.

4 servings

Chicken and Rice Soup

1 — 3 lb. chicken, cut up
7 c. chicken broth
2 stalks celery with tops, cut up
1 medium onion, quartered
2 bay leaves
1/2 tsp. salt
1/4 tsp. pepper
2 carrots, chopped
1 small turnip, chopped
1 c. green beans, cut up
2/3 c. long grain rice
6 oz. cream cheese, cubed

Combine chicken, broth, celery, onion, bay leaves, salt and pepper in dutch oven. Bring to a boil; reduce heat; simmer covered for about 1 hour. Remove chicken; strain broth, discarding vegetables; skim off fat. Return broth to dutch oven, add vegetables and rice. Cover and simmer about 20 minutes until rice is cooked. Remove skin and bones from chicken and cut meat into chunks. Return to soup, add cheese, cook until cheese melts.

8 servings

Vegetable Chili

3 medium onions, sliced
3 stalks celery, sliced
2 green peppers, sliced
4 cloves garlic, minced
2 — 28 oz. cans tomatoes, cut up
3 — 15 oz. cans red kidney beans
1 — 15 oz. can navy beans
1/2 c. raisins
1/2 c. cashews
2 tbsp. oil
1 c. beer
1/4 c. vinegar
1 tbsp. chili powder
1 tbsp. parsley, chopped
2 tsp. salt
1 bay leaf
1 1/2 tsp. basil
1 1/2 tsp. oregano
1/2 tsp. pepper
2 c. shredded cheese

Cook onion, celery, green pepper and garlic in oil until tender. Add all other ingredients except cheese. Bring to a boil, reduce heat and simmer covered for 1 hour. Remove cover and simmer for another hour. Remove bay leaf. Top each serving with 1/4 c. cheese.

8 servings

Capestick Cabbage Soup

1 large cabbage cut in slices
1 c. sliced onions
2 tbsp. butter
3 c. water
4 chicken bouillon cubes
1/4 tsp. white pepper
1/2 tsp. celery salt
2 tbsp. quick cooking tapioca
3 c. milk
1 c. cooked diced ham or bacon

Fry the cabbage and onions in the butter in a large saucepan. Add water, bouillon cubes, pepper, celery salt and simmer for 1 hour. Add topioca and continue simmering for 15 minutes. Add milk and allow to heat without boiling. Add the bacon or ham about 5 minutes before serving.

Serves 8

Salads

Photo taken around 1940

Shrimp and Apple Salad

Mix,
2 apples peeled and diced
8 olives sliced
2 hard boiled eggs sliced
1 tin shrimp
1 green pepper diced

Add 1 tbsp. lemon juice to about 1/4 cup mayonnaise and toss with other ingredients for a few minutes. Serve on lettuce suitably garnished.

Spinach Salad

Dressing:
1/3 c. vegetable oil
3 tbsp. red wine vinegar
1 tbsp. grated Parmesan cheese
1 clove garlic, minced
1/4 tsp. oregano, crushed
1/4 tsp. pepper

Combine all ingredients and chill at least 1 hour before serving. Prepare salad using fresh crisp spinach. Top with sliced hard boiled eggs, and mushrooms, fresh fried crumbled bacon and shredded mozerella cheese. Pour dressing over salad and toss well.

Curried Coleslaw

3 c. shredded cabbage
1/4 c. celery, sliced thin
1/4 c. carrot, shredded
1/4 c. coconut
1/4 c. raisins
2/3 c. mayonnaise
1 tbsp. lemon juice
1 clove garlic, minced
1/2 tsp. curry powder
1/2 c. cashews, chopped coarse

Toss cabbage, celery, carrot, coconut, and raisins in a large bowl. In a separate bowl mix mayonnaise, lemon juice, garlic and curry. Pour over dry ingredients. Toss well to coat. Chill. Add nuts before serving.

6 servings

Halibut Salad

1 lb. halibut seasoned with salt and pepper

Grease a sheet of foil and wrap halibut in it as tightly as possible. Cook in boiling water until fish flakes easily. Reserve all liquid from inside of foil; flake fish and sprinkle with 1 tbsp. of lemon juice. Add enough water to liquid reserved to measure 2 c.; bring to a boil and add

1 chicken bouillon cube.

Soften 1 tbsp. gelatin in 1/4 c. cold water; add to flavored water. Cool until it begins to thicken. Add:

1 c. celery, finely diced
2 tbsp. pimento, chopped
2 tbsp. parsley, chopped
2 tbsp. onion, chopped
1 tsp. salt

Add flaked halibut and pour in a rinsed mold. Chill until firm. Serve on a bed of lettuce.

4 servings

Christmas Salad

2 — 3 oz. pkg. cherry gelatin
1 c. sugar
1 c. water
1/2 c. pineapple juice
1 tbsp. lemon juice
1 orange
2 c. ground cranberries
1 c. thinly sliced celery
1 c. well drained crushed pineapple
1/2 c. coarsely chopped walnuts

Put gelatin and sugar in bowl. Heat water, pineapple juice and lemon juice together. Add to gelatin mixture and stir until dissolved. Chill quickly until just beginning to set. Squeeze orange and add juice to gelatin mixture. Remove all membrane from orange rind and put through fine blade of food processor. Add to gelatin mixture along with the remaining ingredients. Pour into a mold that has been rinsed with cold water. Chill several hours until set. Unmold on lettuce to serve.

6 to 8 servings

Vegetable Salad

1 envelope gelatin
1/4 c. cold water
1 c. hot water
1/4 c. mild vinegar
1 tbsp. lemon juice
1/2 tsp. salt
1 or 2 tbsp. sugar (or more to taste)
    dash of pepper
1 tbsp. finely minced onion (optional)
1 1/2 c. diced or shredded raw or cooked vegetables

Soften gelatin in cold water and dissolve in hot water. Add vinegar, lemon juice, salt, sugar and pepper. Cool. When mixture begins to thicken, fold in vegetables. Turn into a mold or molds that have been rinsed in cold water. When firm unmold on salad greens and serve with desired dressing.

Suggested Combinations:

1 c. shredded raw cabbage, 1/2 c. chopped celery and 2 tbsp. chopped green pepper or pimento
    or
1/2 c. each of cooked peas, diced or shredded raw carrots and celery

Daiquiri Salad

1 c. boiling water
1 — 6 oz. pkg. lime-flavored gelatin
1 — 6 oz. can frozen limeade concentrate
1/2 c. gingerale
20 oz. pineapple tidbits or chunks in juice (drained — reserve
    juice)
4 oz. light rum
    salad greens
    honeydew melon balls

Dissolve the gelatin with hot water in a bowl. Stir in frozen
concentrate. Add enough gingerale to the reserved pineapple
juice to measure 1 1/4 c. Stir in rum and add to the gelatin
mixture. Refrigerate until slightly thickened (approx. 1 hour).
Stir in pineapple. Pour into a rinsed 5 c. mold. Refrigerate
until firm (approx. 3 hours). Unmold on salad greens. Garnish
with melon balls. Serve with whipped cream (optional).

8 to 10 servings

Salmon Salad

2 envelopes unflavored gelatin
1 — 10 oz. can chicken consomme
1 tbsp. lemon juice
1/4 tsp. salt
6 hard boiled eggs
1 lb. salmon
1/4 c. liquid from salmon
1 tsp. minced dry onion
3 oz. chopped mushrooms
1/4 c. water
1/4 c. cider vinegar
2 tsp. sugar
2 tsp. ground marjoram
1 tsp. parsley flakes
1/2 tsp. celery salt
1/4 tsp. ground black pepper
1/2 c. heavy cream, whipped

Sprinkle 1 envelope of gelatin over 1/2 c. of the consomme in a saucepan. Stir until gelatin is dissolved over low heat. Stir in remaining consomme, lemon juice and salt. Pour into bottom of a 6 c. ring mold. Chill until almost firm. Cut eggs in half lengthwise and place in gelatin with yolks face down. Chill until firm. Drain salmon, reserving 1/4 c. of fluid. Remove bones from fish and flake. Add mushrooms and toss lightly. In a saucepan combine salmon liquid, onion, gelatin, water, vinegar, sugar and spices. Cook over low heat; stirring until gelatin is dissolved. Remove from heat and chill until mixture is the consistency of unbeaten egg white. Add salmon mixture and mix well. Fold in whipped cream. Spoon lightly over eggs in ring mold and smoothen. Chill until firm. Fill center with marinated green beens on serving plater.

6 servings

Marinated Green Beans

2 pkg. (10 oz.) frozen cut green beans
2 tbsp. cider vinegar
2 tsp. marjoram
6 tbsp. salad oil
1 tsp. sugar
1/2 tsp. salt
1/4 tsp. pepper

Cook beans until tender crisp. Drain and cool. Combine all other ingredients and blend well. Pour over beans and marinate in refrigerator for about 12 hours.

Lasagna Salad

9 lasagna noodles, cooked and drained
1 1/2 c. green beens, cooked
1/4 c. creamy Italian salad dressing
3 oz. cream cheese, softened
3 tbsp. blue cheese, crumbled
4 oz. cheddar cheese, shredded
3/4 c. cottage cheese, drained
1/3 c. mayonnaise
12 oz. corn, drained
1 1/2 c. bean sprouts, snipped
1 green onion, chopped fine
2 small tomatoes, peeled and sliced thin

Mix beans and corn together. Combine cream and blue cheese with salad dressing and mayonnaise. Stir about 1/3 of this mixture in with the beans and corn. Combine about 3/4 c. of the shredded cheddar with the cottage cheese, onion and bean sprouts. Place half the lasagna noodle in bottom of a large shallow baking dish. Top with tomatoes and bean sprout mixture. Place remainder of noodles on top and cover with green bean mixture. Sprinkle with the remaining cheddar. Cover and chill.

8 servings

Fruit Salad Ring

1 envelope gelatin
1/4 c. cold water
1/4 c. lemon juice
1 1/2 c. leftover canned or fresh fruits
1 c. hot fruit juice or water
1/4 c. sugar
1/4 tsp. salt

Soften gelatin in cold water and dissolve in hot fruit juice (drained from canned fruits) or water. Add lemon juice, sugar and salt. Cool and when mixture begins to thicken, fold in diced fruits. Any fruits or desired combinations may be used. Pour into a mold that has been rinsed with cold water or individual molds. Chill. When firm, unmold on lettuce; serve with mayonnaise or fruit dressing.

6 servings

Hot Spinach Salad

4 c. spinach, torn
2 hard boiled eggs, sliced
1/2 c. mushrooms, sliced
6 slices of bacon, fried crisp and crumbled
1 small onion, diced coarse
1/4 c. apple juice
3 tbsp. wine vinegar
1 tbsp. brown sugar
1 1/2 tsp. cornstarch
1 tbsp. cooking oil

Combine apple juice, wine vinegar, brown sugar, and corn starch. Place spinach in serving bowl. In a skillet saute onion in oil for a couple of minutes, add mushrooms and fry for a couple more minutes. Push vegetables to the outside of pan and add liquid to center. Stir and cook until thickened. Stir vegetables in sauce and add bacon. Continue to cook for another minute. Pour over spinach and toss gently. Top with egg slices and grated parmesan cheese if desired.

3 servings

Spicy Cabbage

1/2 red cabbage, coarsely shredded
1 apple, sliced
1 onion, sliced thin
1/2 c. dry red wine
1/4 c. red wine vinegar
1/4 c. apple jelly
2 tbsp. margarine
1 tbsp. cornstarch
2 whole cloves

Melt margarine in saucepan over medium heat. Cook apple and onion until soft but not mushy. Add all remaining ingredients except cornstarch. Heat to boiling and reduce heat. Cook approx. 30 minutes or until cabbage is tender. Drain, reserving liquid. Mix 2 tbsp. of the liquid with the cornstarch. Gradually stir in the remainder of the liquid and smoothen. Return to saucepan. Boil for about 1 minute stirring constantly. Pour over cabbage.

4 servings

Salad

1 quart kraut, washed, drain well
1 can crushed pineapple drained
1 onion sliced
1 green pepper in strips
2 cups celery — chopped
1 cup red pepper (or 1 cup grated carrot)
2 cups sugar dissolved in 1 cup vinegar

Pour over vegetables. Keep in fridge.

Marinated Carrot Salad

2 lbs. carrot
1 large onion
1 green pepper
1 — 10 oz. can tomato soup
1 cup sugar
3/4 c. vinegar
1/2 c. salad oil
1/2 tsp. dry mustard
1 tsp. salt
pepper

Cook carrots until just barely done. Slice onion and green pepper and add to cooked, drained carrots. Bring sauce to a boil and pour over the vegetables. Refrigerate. This keeps for weeks.

Potatoes

2 lbs. new potatoes
1/4 c. margarine
1/4 c. sugar
1/2 tsp. salt
3 tbsp. water

Heat 1" salted water (1 tsp. salt to 1 c. water) to boiling. Add potatoes and cook 25 minutes till tender. Drain. Cook and stir margarine, sugar and salt in large skillet over medium until mixture begins to turn golden brown. Remove from heat and cool slightly. Stir in water until blended. Add potatoes. Cook over low heat, turning potatoes to coat.

Hot Potato Salad

8 potatoes — peeled, cooked and sliced 1/4" thick
4 slices bacon
1/2 c chopped onion
1 1/2 tsp. flour
4 tsp. sugar
1/4 tsp. pepper
1/3 c. white vinegar
1/2 c. water
1/4 c. minced onion
1/4 c. sweet pickle relish
1/2 c. sliced radish

Cut bacon in small pieces and cook slowly in frying pan until crisp. Saute onion in bacon fat. Combine flour, sugar, pepper and stir into bacon fat. Add combined vinegar and water and cook until slightly thickened. Add minced onion, relish and radish. Pour over sliced potatoes. Serve lightly tossed and garnished with celery leaves.

Makes 4-6 servings

Breads

Photo taken around 1940

Freezer Chicken Salad Rolls

8 hot dog rolls
1 cup diced, cooked chicken
1 stalks celery (diced)
2 oz. Mild cheese (such as Swiss)
1/2 cup drained, crushed pineapple
1/8 tsp. salt
1/4 c. mayonnaise
pepper

Butter rolls. Mix ingredients and put about 1/4 cup mixture in each roll. Wrap separately if they are to be frozen. Thaw in wrapper. Will keep about two months in freezer. Warm in oven before serving.

Clover Leaf Rolls

1 pint scalded milk
2 tbsp. butter
2 tbsp. sugar
1 1/2 tsp. salt

Mix and cool to lukewarm. Add:

1 yeast cake dissolved in
1/4 c. lukewarm water
1 egg white, beaten stiff
6 c. of flour

This recipe required about 3 hours to rise. Then place 3 small balls of dough in each hole of muffin pan with a piece of butter in between each one. Allow to rise until about double in bulk. Bake in moderate oven 20 to 25 minutes.

Overnight Rolls

(Makes six or seven dozen)
Begin to mix rolls at 4 or 5 o'clock in afternoon. Beat 3 eggs.
Add 2/3 cup sugar, 3/4 cup cooking oil, 1 tbsp. salt, 1 tbsp.
yeast dissolved in 1/4 cup warm water, 4 cups warm water, 12
cups (or little more) flour. Mix well and knead till smooth. Put
to rise in warm place. At 7 p.m. and 8 or 8:30 p.m. punch down
and knead a few turns. At 10 p.m. make into rolls (size of silver
dollar). Cover with waxed paper and leave overnight. Bake
first thing in the morning in a 400°F oven.

Brown Bread

1 c. rolled oats
2 tsp. salt
1 1/2 tbsp. shortening
1 3/4 c. boiling water (let stand until lukewarm)
3/4 c. brown sugar
2 tbsp. molasses
2 c. flour
2 1/2 c. flour

Measure in a bowl:
1/2 c. warm water
2 tsp. sugar
2 pkg. dry yeast

Yeast Breads

White bread or rolls:
1 1/2 c. water
1/2 c. milk
3 tbsp. honey
2 tsp. salt
3 tbsp. margarine or shortening

— — — — — — — — —

1/2 c. lukewarm water
1 tsp. honey
1 tbsp. dry yeast
6 or 7 c. flour

Scald 1 1/2 c. water and milk. Stir in honey, salt and margarine. Cool to lukewarm. Dissolve 1 tsp. honey and yeast in 1/2 c. lukewarm water. Let stand 10 minutes. Stir and add to the first mixture. Add 3 c. flour and beat until smooth. Stir in enough flour to make a soft dough. Turn mixture out onto a lightly floured board. Knead until smooth and elastic (approx. 10 minutes). Place in a greased bowl, turning to grease the top as well. Cover and let rise in a warm area until doubled in bulk. Punch down and turn dough out on a lightly floured board. Cover and allow to rise for 15 minutes. Place in pans. Cover and allow to rise for a further 45 minutes. Bake at 400°F for 25 to 30 minutes. Cool on racks.

Chelsea Rolls

Dough:
1/2 c. milk
1/4 c. sugar
1 tsp. salt
1/2 c. lukewarm water
1 tsp. sugar
1 envelope dry yeast
1 egg well beaten
3 1/2 c. sifted flour
1/4 c. shortening softened

Filling and Glaze:
soft butter or margarine
3/4 c. lightly packed brown sugar
2 tsp. ground cinnamon
1/2 c. seedless raisins
2/3 c. lightly packed brown sugar

Scald milk. Stir in sugar and salt. Cool to lukewarm. Meantime measure lukewarm water into large bowl and stir in 1 tsp. sugar. Sprinkle with yeast. Let stand 10 minutes then stir well. Stir in lukewarm milk mixture, egg, 2 cups of the flour and soft shortening. Beat until smooth and elastic. Work in remaining flour. Knead dough until smooth and elastic. Place in greased bowl. Grease top — cover. Let rise in warm draft-free area until doubled in bulk (approximately 1 1/2 hours). Punch down dough. Knead until smooth. Halve dough and roll each half into 9" square. Brush with soft butter or margarine. Combine 3/4 cup brown sugar, cinnamon and seedless raisins. Sprinkle over dough. Roll in a jelly roll fashion and cut each roll into 6 slices. Melt 1 tbsp. butter or margarine in each of 2 loaf pans and brush sides of pans with fat and sprinkle 1/3 c. brown sugar in each pan. Place 6 rolls — cut sides up — in each pan. Grease tops. Cover. Let rise until double in bulk (about 1/2 hour). Bake in 375ºF oven 1/2 hour.
Makes 12 buns

Bread

15 c. flour
6 tbsp. sugar
3 tbsp. salt
1 yeast cake dissolved in 1/2 c. warm water with 1 tsp. sugar
6 c. lukewarm water to melt shortening 5 or 6 tbsp.

Allow to raise overnight.

4 loaves

Sultana Scones

3 c. flour
1 tsp. cream of tartar
1/2 tsp. baking soda
1 tsp. salt
1 c. shortening
1/2 c. white sugar
1 egg beaten
1/2 c. milk
1/2 c. raisins

Roll 1/2 inch thick. Brush top with milk. Bake at 425°F for 15 minutes.

Never Fail Fluffy Biscuits

Sift together into a bowl:
2 c. flour
2 tsp. sugar
1/4 tsp. cream of tartar
4 tsp. baking powder
1/2 tsp. salt

Add: 1/2 c. shortening

Cut shortening into dry mixture with a pastry blender, 2 knives or mix with your fingers until the mixture looks like coarse cornmeal. Add all at one time: 2/3 c. milk. Stir just enough to make a soft dough. Turn out onto a lightly floured board. Kneed lightly for 30 seconds. Roll out to a thickness of 1/2 inch. Cut with a floured 2 inch round cutter. Place on an ungreased baking sheet. Bake at 450°F for 12-15 minutes.

Banana Muffins

1 c. pancake mix powder
2 tbsp. sugar
1/2 tsp. pumpkin pie spice
1 small banana, mashed
approx. 1/3 c. milk

Mix dry ingredients. Add banana and enough milk to make a thick batter. Fill greased muffin cups approximately 2/3 full. Bake at 375°F for 15 minutes.

6 muffins

Blueberry Muffins

1 c. white sugar
2 eggs
2 c. flour
2 tsp. baking powder
1 tsp. vanilla
1/2 c. margarine
1/2 c. milk
1/2 tsp. salt
2 c. blueberries

Stir together all dry ingredients. Add blueberries. Combine melted butter, eggs and milk and stir into flour mixture. Stir only enough to moisten. Do not beat. Bake at 375^{0}F for 20 minutes.

Savory Gems

2 c. flour
1 1/4 c. grated cheese
1 1/8 c. water
   pinch of white pepper
2 tbsp. baking powder
2 tbsp. shortening
1/2 tsp. dry mustard
1/2 tsp. salt

Mix dry ingredients. Cut in shortening. Add cheese and the liquid. Place by spoonfulls in muffin tins. Bake at 375^0 to 400^{0}F.

Cranberry Muffins

1 3/4 c. flour
1/2 c. sugar
1 tbsp. baking powder
1 tsp. salt
2 eggs, well beaten
3/4 c. milk
1/3 c. salad oil
1 c. fresh or frozen cranberries

Preheat oven to 350⁰F. Sift flour, sugar, baking powder and salt into a large bowl and set aside. Combine egg, milk, and oil. Mix well and add to the dry ingredients. Stir until just moistened. Fold in cranberries. Bake for 25-30 minutes or until done.

Block-Buster Bran Muffins

1/4 c. light vegetable oil
1/4 c. molasses
1/4 c. maple syrup (or brown sugar)
2 eggs (beaten)
1 c. milk
3/4 c. flour
1/4 c. wheat germ
1 1/2 tsp. baking powder
1/2 tsp. baking soda
3/4 tsp. salt
1 1/2 c. natural wheat bran
2/3 c. fruit (mixed if desired: raisins, dates, figs, apple, berries, etc.)

Mix oil, molasses, maple syrup and eggs. Beat together well. Add milk and then bran. Mix. Combine flour, wheat germ, baking powder, soda and salt. Add to liquids. Add fruit. Place in greased muffin pans. Bake in 400⁰F oven for 18-20 minutes.
Makes 12 large muffins.

Jenny's Crunchy Granola

1 1/2 lbs. rolled oats
1 c. wheat germ
1/2 c. sesame seeds
1 c. coconut
1 c. sunflower seeds
1 c. raisins, appricots
1 c. nuts (almonds, pecans, cashews)
1/2 tsp. salt
1/2 c. demerera sugar or brown
1/2 c. honey — unpasteurized
1/2 c. water
1/2 peanut oil or light veg. oil
1/2 tsp. vanilla
1/2 tsp. cinnamon

Mix all dry ingredients. Sprinkle wet ingredients over dry and knead with fingers. On large flat trays cook in oven at 375⁰F for 30-60 minutes. Then add flavours.

Bran Muffins

1 c. flour
1 tsp. baking soda
1/2 tsp. salt
1 c. all-bran
1/2 c. raisins, dates, apple, etc.
2 tbsp. shortening
1/2 c. molasses
3/4 c. hot water
1 egg (beaten)

Measure and sift flour, baking soda and salt into large bowl. In another bowl measure bran, molasses, raisins, shortening and water. Stir until shortening is dissolved then add egg. Mix well. Combine wet and dry ingredients. Fill muffin tins 2/3 full. Bake 425⁰F, about 20 min.
(If natural bran is used, add extra liquid.)

Makes 12 large muffins

Doughnuts

1 1/2 c. white sugar
2 tbsp. shortening, margarine or butter
4 eggs — beaten
1 tsp. vanilla
2 tsp. lemon
1 tsp. salt
1 tsp. soda
1 tsp. ginger
2 tsp. nutmeg
1 tsp. cream of tartar
2 tsp. baking powder
1 c. milk
6 c. all purpose flour

Cream the sugar and butter well. Add the beaten eggs and 2 cups of flour. Add the remaining ingredients with the milk. Finally add the remaining 4 cups of flour. Fry in deep fat.

Yield — 5 to 6 dozen

Cinnamon Buns

1 c. warm water
2 pkg. active dry yeast (or 2 tbsp.)
1/2 c. milk
1/2 c. white sugar
1 1/2 tsp. salt
2 tsp. white sugar
1/4 c. butter or margarine
2 eggs, well beaten
5 1/2 c. (approx.) all purpose flour
1 1/2 c. brown sugar
2 tsp. cinnamon
2/3 c. seedless raisins
   melted butter

Pour water in a large bowl; stir in 2 tsp. sugar and yeast. Let stand 10 minutes. Over low heat, combine milk, 1/2 c. sugar, 1/4 c. butter and salt. Heat until butter melts. Cool to lukewarm. Add to yeast solution. Add eggs and 1 1/2 c. flour. Stir in enough of the remaining flour to make a soft dough. Place in a greased bowl; cover with a damp cloth and allow to rise until doubled in bulk. Turn out on a lightly floured board. Divide in half. Roll each half into a rectangle approx. 18 X 9. Brush with melted butter. Combine raisins, brown sugar and cinnamon. Sprinkle half the mixture on each of the two rectangles. Roll up jelly roll fashion. Cut each roll in 12 pieces about 1 1/2 inches thick. Place with cut side up in 2 X 9 inch round cake pans. Allow to rise about 1 hour. Bake 30 minutes at 350°F.

Pear and Nut Loaf

2 or 3 fresh pears
1/2 c. salad oil
1 c. sugar
2 eggs
1/4 c. sour milk
1 tsp. vanilla
2 c. all-purpose flour
1/2 tsp. salt
1 tsp. soda
1/4 tsp. cinnamon
1/4 tsp. nutmeg
1/2 c. walnuts

Pare, halve and core pears and chop to make one cup. In large bowl beat together oil and sugar until well blended. Beat in eggs, one at a time, the sour milk and vanilla. Sift flour, salt, soda and spices. Add to oil mixture and beat to blend. Bake in 9" X 5" loaf pan in 350°F oven for one hour.

Banana Bread

1 c. white sugar
1/2 c. shortening
1 c. bananas
2 c. flour
1 tsp. soda
   pinch of salt or 1/2 tsp.
2 eggs beaten
1/2 c. chopped nuts

Cream sugar and shortening. Add remaining ingredients. Bake at 350°F for 1 hour.

Chocolate Chip Loaf

1/2 c. margarine
1 c. sugar
2 eggs (beaten)
juice of 1 orange, plus milk to make 1 cup
1 tsp. vanilla
2 c. flour
1 tsp. baking powder
1/2 tsp. salt
3 oz. chocolate chips
1/2 c. walnuts
1/2 c. cherries

Cream margarine and sugar; add eggs and juice, mix well. Add dry ingredients. Also dusted chips, cherries and nuts. Bake at 350⁰F for 50-60 minutes or until toothpick inserted in centre comes out dry.

Cherry Orange Bread

2 1/2 c. sifted all purpose flour
3 1/2 tsp. baking powder
3/4 tsp. salt
1 1/2 tsp. cinnamon
1/2 tsp. nutmeg
2/3 c. sugar
1/2 lb. chopped candied cherries
1/4 lb. chopped citron peel
2 tsp. grated orange rind
2 eggs
1 1/4 c. milk
2 tbsp. melted shortening

Sift together flour, baking powder, salt, spices and sugar. Stir in fruits and grated orange rind until well coated with flour. Combine well beaten eggs, milk and shortening and stir into the dry ingredients just until blended. Pour into a greased loaf pan and allow to stand for 15 minutes. Bake at 350⁰F for 60 to 70 minutes. Brush bread while still hot with hot corn syrup and garnish with bits of candied fruit.

Fish

Mackerel fishing

Broiled Mackerel

1 small mackerel per person
butter, lemon pepper (or lemon juice and black pepper)
salt and garlic powder

Turn oven to low broil. Place mackerel on rack in broiler pan skin down. Spread generously with butter and season with lemon pepper, a dash of salt and garlic powder. Broil until fish flakes easily, about 10-15 minutes. Baste once or twice with juices in pan. Serve with tossed salad.

Haddock Scalloped au Gratin

1 lb. haddock
2 oz. margarine
1/2 green pepper minced
1/2 onion minced
1/2 tsp. salt
1/8 tsp. pepper
1/2 c. grated or crumbled cheese
1/2 c. cracker crumbs
1 c. milk
2 tbsp. flour
1/2 tsp. worcestershire sauce

Wash haddock and cut into cubes. Melt butter in saucepan. Add minced pepper, onion, fish cubes, salt and pepper and gently saute over low heat ten minutes or until pepper is half done. Blend milk and flour until smooth. Put in top of double boiler and cook ten minutes or until sauce begins to thicken. Stir in worcestershire sauce and haddock. Mix well. Pour into greased casserole. Combine cheese and crackers and spread over fish. Bake at 300⁰F for 10 minutes or until golden brown.

Fish and Biscuits

1 lb. haddock fillets
1 c. chicken stock
1 stalk celery, sliced
1 carrot, sliced
1 onion, chopped
2 tbsp. margarine or butter
2 tbsp. flour
1/4 c. cold water
1/2 tsp. summer savory
salt and pepper tò taste
1 c. peas

In medium saucepan bring stock and vegetables to a boil. Simmer for five minutes. Add fish. Simmer for ten minutes. Remove fish and set aside. Strain and measure stock. (Should have 1 1/4 cups) Return stock to pan. Heat. Add butter. Make thin paste of flour and cold water. Stir into a hot stock and simmer until thickened. Add seasonings, peas and fish. Put into 6 cup casserole. Make biscuit topping of the following:

1 c. flour
2 tsp. baking flour
1 tsp. salt
3 tbsps. shortening
1 tbsp. chopped parsley
1/2 c. milk

Drop by spoonfulls on hot fish mixture. Bake in 425^{0}F oven for about 25 minutes.

Fish and Broccoli Casserole

1 c. flaked fish
1 package (10 oz.) frozen broccoli spears, cooked 3 minutes
and drained
1 can (10 oz.) cream of mushroom soup
1/2 c. milk
1/4 tsp. salt
1/8 tsp. pepper
1/2 c. crushed potato chips

Place cooked broccoli spears in a single layer, in a well greased
shallow casserole. Combine fish, soup, milk, salt and pepper,
spread over broccoli spears, sprinkle potato chips over top.
Bake at 425^{0}F for 10-12 minutes or until hot.

Lemon Butter Flavoured Fish

2 lb. fillets
1/2 tsp. salt
1/2 tsp. marjoram
1/4 tsp. paprika
1/8 tsp. pepper
1/4 c. melted butter
2 lemons, sliced thin

Cut fillets in serving size portions. Arrange in a greased baking
dish. Stir seasonings into melted butter. Combine well.
Spread evenly over fillets. Top with lemon slices. Bake at
450^{0}F for 10 minutes per inch for fresh fish and 20 minutes per
inch for thickness for frozen fish. Baste fish occasionally with
cooking liquid while baking.

6 servings

Court Bouillon for Poaching Fish

2 1/2 c. water
3/4 tsp. salt
1/2 c. dry white wine (or 3 tbsp. lemon juice may be
    substituted)
1/3 c. thinly sliced carrot
1 stalk thinly sliced celery
1 small onion chopped
1 small bay leaf
3 or 4 peppercorns
1/4 tsp. thyme
2 or 3 whole cloves

Put all ingredients in saucepan or covered skillet. Bring to a
boil. Simmer for about 10 minutes, then add fish, and simmer
gently until fish flakes with a fork. This will do about 1 lb. mild
fish such as salmon or haddock or cod. Bouillon may be
strained and use in making sauce for fish or store in airtight jar
for later use.

Poached Fish

1 lb. fish fillets
1 medium onion, sliced
3 slices lemon
3 sprigs parsley
1 bay leaf
1 tsp. salt
2 peppercorns

In large skillet, heat to boiling 1 1/2" water with all ingredients
except fish. Arrange fish in a single layer in skillet; cover and
simmer 5 minutes or until fish flakes easily with a fork.

3 servings

Haddock a la George

In a large cast iron skillet, saute

1/2 lb. butter
2 onions, chopped
6 carrots, chopped
3 potatoes, halved
3 celery stalks, chopped

Lay a cleaned haddock on this bed of vegetables. Combine the following ingredients and pour over the haddock:

1/2 c. grapefruit juice
6 tbsp. wine or beer
juice of 1 lemon
salt and pepper
1 tsp. green spices
1/2 garlic, crushed
4 slivers of ginger
lemon rind

Simmer until cooked.

Devilled Fish

2 lb. haddock fillets
1 lb. scallops

Grease top of a double boiler. Put scallops in first and cover with haddock. Cover pan and steam 20 minutes. Cool and cut in bite-size pieces. Melt 8 tbsp. butter (margarine) and blend in 9 tbsp. flour. Heat 1 c. undiluted evaporated milk, 1 1/2 c. whole milk and 1 c. consomme. Add hot liquid to flour and butter mixture and stir smooth. Let thicken, stirring on low heat. Add:

1 tbsp. lemon juice
1 tbsp. worcestershire sauce
1 tbsp. horseradish
1 lg. clove of garlic, grated
1 tsp. prepared mustard
1/2 tsp. salt
1 tsp. soya sauce
4 tbsp. minced parsley
1/4 c. sherry

Stir sauce well and add fish gently. Turn into a greased shallow casserole. Sprinkle with buttered bread crumbs. This can be kept refrigerated until the next day. Heat through thoroughly in a hot oven before serving.

8 servings

Baked Haddock

Clean and scale a 3 to 4 lb. haddock. Remove fins and wash well. Pat dry with paper towel. Fill the fish with dressing. Shake a bit of flour over the fish. Cut bacon in strips and lay over the haddock. Bake until done at 350°F.

Bread Stuffing (for 4 lb. fish)

3 c. soft bread crumbs
2 oz. butter
1 small onion, minced
1/4 tsp. rosemary
1/4 c. milk
1/2 tsp. salt
1/8 tsp. pepper
1/2 tsp. thyme

Melt butter in saucepan, add onion and saute over low heat 5 minutes or until light brown. Remove from heat. Add salt, pepper, rosemary and thyme. Blend well. Put bread crumbs in large bowl. Add blended seasonings. Mix well. Add only enough milk to moisten slightly.

Variations:
Celery stuffing — omit milk and add 1 cup chopped raw celery.
Cheese stuffing — add 1 c. grated mild cheese.

Baked Fish

2 lb. fish fillets
1/2 c. undiluted evaporated milk
1 tsp. salt
1 tsp. lemon juice
2 c. cereal, crushed
1 tbsp. butter

Cut fillets in serving portions; soak in mixture of milk, lemon juice and salt. Roll in cereal crumbs and place in a greased baking dish. Dot with butter. Bake at 450°F approximately 10 minutes per inch of thickness for fresh fish. Double the cooking time if the fish is frozen.

Salmon Loaf

2 c. salmon
1/2 c. fresh bread crumbs
4 tbsp. melted butter
2 eggs, well beaten
1 1/2 tbsp. minced onion
2 tsp. minced parsley
1 tbsp. minced green pepper
1/4 tsp. worcestershire sauce
dash of tabasco
salt

Preheat oven to 350°F and grease 1 qt. loaf pan. Combine all ingredients. Mix well and press into loaf pan. Bake for 30 minutes.

Salmon Luncheon Roll

1 lb. salmon, cooked and flaked
1/2 c. celery, chopped
1/4 c. green pepper, chopped
1/4 c. onion, chopped
1/2 c. cheese, grated
1 tsp. dill weed
1/2 tsp. tarragon
mayonnaise (enough to moisten mixture — 1/4 c.)
pastry (sufficient for a double crust)
salt and pepper
milk; or juice from salmon if using canned fish

Mix first 7 ingredients well. Roll pastry to shape a tube, approximately 12 X 5. Spread salmon mixture evenly over the pastry, leaving about 1/2 inch bare on one long edge. Start from the opposite edge and roll jelly roll fashion; seal pastry with water. Make some small slits in the top of pastry roll for steam to escape. Brush with milk (or salmon juice). Bake at 375°F for approximately 1/2 hour; until pastry is cooked.

4 servings

Salmon with Tarragon Sauce

4 salmon steaks
1 c. water
1/4 c. dry white wine
2 lemon slices
1 bay leaf
1/4 tsp. salt
1 tbsp. butter
1 tbsp. flour
1/4 tsp. tarragon
1 egg yolk, beaten
salt

In a greased large frying pan add wine, lemon, bay leaf and salt. Bring to a boil, add fish and simmer, covered until fish flakes easily. Remove fish (keep warm); stir in liquid, reserving 3/4 c. Melt butter in a saucepan, stir in flour and cook over low heat. Add fish stock, tarragon and salt to taste. Cook until thickened. Slowly stir 1/4 c. of mixture into egg yolk. Return to remainder of hot liquid. Cook, stirring constantly for another few minutes till thick. Spoon over salmon.

4 servings

Scallops in Wine Sauce

1 1/2 lbs. scallops (frozen)
1 small onion, chopped
1/4 c. parsley
2 c. dry white wine
2 tbsp. margarine
2 c. sliced mushrooms
1 shallot, chopped
3 tbsp. margarine
2 tbsp. flour
2 tbsp. cream
4 oz. Gruyere cheese, grated
2 tbsp. margarine
1 c. soft bread crumbs

Place scallops, onion and parsley in 3 qt. saucepan. Add wine to just cover scallops. Heat to boiling. Reduce heat. Simmer uncovered until scallops are tender (about 8 minutes). Drain scallops. Reserve liquid. Heat to boiling and boil until reduced to 1 c. (30 minutes). Strain and reserve. Heat 2 tbsp. margarine in skillet till melted. Add mushrooms, shallot and cook until shallot is tender (6 minutes). Heat 3 tbsp. margarine in 1 1/2 qt. saucepan — stir in flour and reserved scallop-wine liquid; beat until smooth. Cook over low heat, stirring constantly until sauce is medium thick. Remove from heat. Stir in cream, scallops, mushrooms and 1/4 c. cheese. Spoon mixture into five buttered baking shells or ramekins. Sprinkle with remaining. Set oven to broil or 550⁰. Broil 5" from heat until bubbly (4 or 5 minutes). Heat 2 tbsp. margarine until melted add crumbs and toss. Sprinkle over scallops. Broil until crumbs are toasted.

5 servings

Scallops Oven-Fried

2 lb. scallops
2 eggs
2 tbsp. water
1/2 tsp. thyme
1/4 tsp. dill
1 c. cracker crumbs
2 oz. butter, melted
4 tsp. chopped chives
salt and pepper

Wipe scallops with a damp cloth. Break eggs into a mixing bowl and beat until foamy. Add water; season with spices and mix well. Dip scallops in egg mixture and then roll in cracker crumbs. Place scallops in a greased shallow baking dish or on scallop shells. Pour melted butter over the scallops. Bake at 450°F for 20 minutes. Serve over buttered toast.

6 servings

Stir Fry Scallops

1 lb. scallops (cut any large ones in half)
2 c. shredded unpeeled zucchini
2 tbsp. oil
1/4 c. water
2 tbsp. herbed mustard
2 tsp. lemon juice
1 tsp. cornstarch
3 tbsp. cashews

Steam zucchini over water for about 2 minutes. Remove from heat but keep over hot water to keep hot while preparing the scallops. Stir fry the scallops, half at a time, in oil. Remove. Mix the remaining ingredients together and add to wok. Cook, stirring until thickened and bubbly. Cook for a further 2 minutes. Spoon scallops over zucchini; top with any remaining sauce and sprinkle with chopped nuts.

4 servings

Finnan Haddie Baked in Milk

2 lb. smoked haddock
4 tbsp. butter
1 onion, thinly sliced
1/2 tsp. pepper
1 c. milk
1 bay leaf
1/8 tsp. nutmeg
Cayenne pepper

Soak haddock in warm water for about 1 hour. Grease a shallow baking dish. Place drained fish in dish. Preheat oven to 375°F. Melt butter in skillet and cook onion over medium heat until tender. Stir in remaining ingredients and pour mixture over fish. Bake for 45 minutes.

Golden Curried Scallops

1 lb. scallops
salt
1/4 c. fine dry bread crumbs
3 tbsp. butter or margarine
2 tbsp. lemon juice
1 tsp. curry powder
1/2 lemon cut in thin slices

Separate scallops, salt and roll in bread crumbs. Arrange in shallow greased baking dish (or on scallop shells). Melt fat, add lemon juice and curry powder. Blend well and pour over scallops. Top with lemon slices. Bake at 450°F for 15 minutes.

4 servings

Mussel Casserole

2 c. mussel meat
3/4 lb. cooked noodles
1/2 c. butter
1 c. mushrooms, sliced
2 tbsp. green pepper, chopped
1/4 c. onion, diced
6 tbsp. flour
4 c. milk
3/4 c. dry white wine
2 1/2 c. Swiss cheese, grated
paprika
salt and pepper

Put mussels and noodles in a large casserole. Melt butter over medium heat in frying pan; add mushrooms, onion and green pepper; cook until tender. Remove from heat and take vegetables from pan with a slotted spoon. Add flour to butter remaining in the pan over low heat. Add salt and pepper to taste, stirring constantly until thick. Remove from heat, stir in wine and pour the sauce over the mussel noodle vegetable mixture. Toss, sprinkle with cheese and colour with paprika. Bake uncovered in preheated oven at 350°F for 45 minutes.

6 servings

Seafood Lasagna

1 1/2 lb. cod fillets
6 lasagna noodles, cooked
1 lb. mozzarella cheese, sliced
1/4 c. parmesan cheese
1 lg. tub cottage cheese
1 medium onion, diced
1/3 c. green pepper, diced
2 tbsp. butter
1 — 14 oz. can tomato sauce
1/2 tsp. salt
1/2 tsp. basil
pepper
1/2 tsp. oregano
1/4 tsp. Italian seasoning

Cut fish in bite-size pieces. Stir fry onion, pepper in butter until tender. Stir in tomato sauce and seasonings. Simmer for about 5 minutes. Add fish and continue to simmer a further 5 minutes. Sprinkle a little of the mixture over the bottom of a greased baking dish (12 X 8). Place a layer of lasagna noodles in dish; cover with sauce mixture, then cottage cheese, parmesan cheese and mozzarella. Repeat. Top with a layer of mozzarella. Bake at 350⁰F for 20 to 25 minutes until bubbly and lightly browned. Freezing enhances flavour.

6 servings

Creamed Cod

1 1/2 lb. cod
1 1/2 c. heavy cream
5 tbsp. flour
1 1/2 tsp. salt
1/4 tsp. pepper
1/2 tsp. tarragon
2 tbsp. chives, finely chopped
2 tbsp. parsley, minced
3 tbsp. lemon juice

Preheat oven to 450°F. Add salt and pepper to flour and roll fish in it. Place in a greased baking dish. Sprinkle with tarragon, chives, parsley and lemon juice. Pour cream over fish and bake about 15 minutes.

4 servings

Creamed Lobster

5 tbsp. butter
5 tbsp. flour
2 c. light cream
1/2 tsp. nutmeg
pinch of cayenne pepper
3 tbsp. lemon juice
2 c. cooked lobster meat
toast or patty shells
1 tbsp. finely chopped parsley

Melt butter in saucepan. Stir in flour and cook over low heat. Slowly add cream, stirring constantly. Add nutmeg, cayenne pepper and lemon juice. Cook, stirring until the sauce is smooth and thickened. Add lobster and heat thoroughly. Spoon over toast or patty shells. Garnish with parsley.

Codfish Cakes

1 lb. salt cod (soaked out)
3 c. mashed potatoes
1/3 c. cream
4 tbsp. softened butter
1/2 tsp. pepper

Simmer fish for ten minutes in enough water to cover. Drain. Flake the fish. Add remaining ingredients and mix well. Shape into small cakes and fry in oil until golden brown without allowing them to touch.

Fish Fritters

1 1/2 lbs. cod, haddock, or Boston bluefish, cooked and flaked
1 c. flour
1 tsp. baking powder
1 egg slightly beaten
3/4 c. milk
1/4 c. chopped green onion (including top)
1/2 c. mushrooms finely chopped
1 c. grated cheddar cheese
Vegetable oil for deep frying

Blend flour, baking powder, egg and milk together with a whisk. Add the fish and the remaining ingredients and mix well. Heat oil to 370ºF (185ºC). Place spoonfulls of batter in heated fat. Fry until golden brown — about 5 minutes. Serve with lemon.

Seafood Newburg

1/2 c. butter
1/2 c. flour
4 c. milk (or 3 c. milk and 1 can cream of shrimp soup)
2 tsp. minced onion
1 tsp. dry mustard
2 tsp. parsley flakes
6 tbsp. sherry
2 tsp. worcestershire sauce
1/2 c. chopped pimento
2 — 7 oz. cans tuna
2 — 4 1/2 oz. cans shrimp
2 — 6 oz. cans lobster or crab meat

Melt butter in saucepan and gradually add flour stirring constantly. Add onion and mustard and parsley flakes. Add milk and cook and stir until thickened to a creamy consistency. Remove from heat and add sherry, worcestershire and pimento. Fold in fish which has been drained and flaked. Pour into buttered casserole. Bake at 350°F for about 45 minutes. Garnish with chow mein noodles.

Fried Lobster

1 1/2 lbs. lobster meat cut in large cubes
1/4 tsp. oregano
paprika
4 oz. butter
2 tbsp. sherry
salt

Melt butter in frying pan over medium. When hot add oregano and lobster. Lower heat slightly. Cover pan five minutes allowing lobster to heat thoroughly. Remove cover and continue frying five minutes over higher heat until crispy brown on all sides, stirring constantly to brown evenly. Remove lobster and place on preheated individual plates. Quickly add sherry and pinch of salt to butter in pan. Boil one minute. Pour steaming hot over lobster. Sprinkle with dash of paprika.

Scallop Bake

1 lb. scallops (salt water)
2 tbsp. butter
1/2 c. chopped onions
1 c. sliced mushrooms
1 c. chopped green pepper
1 1/2 c. chopped celery
1-2 c. soft bread crumbs
1-2 tbsp. melted butter
1/4 c. finely grated cheddar cheese

Sauce

1/4 c. butter
1/4 c. flour
1 tsp. salt
2 c. milk

Separate scallops and sprinkle with salt. Melt in frypan 2 tbsp. butter and pan fry onions, mushrooms, green pepper, celery until partly cooked (10 min.). Don't cook until limp. Make medium white sauce by combining and cooking 1/4 c. butter, 1/4 c. flour, 1 tsp. salt and 2 c. milk. When thickened, add above vegetables and scallops and mix well. Place in 1 1/2 qt. casserole dish (greased). Mix the 1-2 tbsp. of melted butter with bread crumbs and spread on top of above, then sprinkle cheese on top and place in 375⁰F oven. Bake until you notice edges bubbling and bread crumbs are slightly brown (approx. 20 min.).

Seafood Coquille

8 oz. crabmeat
1 c. cooked shrimp
1/2 c. Swiss cheese, shredded
2/3 c. sauterne
1 1/3 c. milk
1/3 c. butter
1/3 c. minced onion
1 clove garlic, crushed
1/4 c. flour
salt and pepper

Cook onion and garlic in melted butter. Remove from heat and blend in flour and salt and pepper. Cook over low heat, stirring until mixture is bubbly. Stir in wine and milk. Heat to boiling stirring constantly. Boil and stir about 1 minute. Stir in crabmeat and shrimp. Turn into 4 baking dishes. Sprinkle each with cheese. Broil about 4 inches from heat until cheese is golden.

4 servings

Scallop and Lobster Casserole

1 lb. scallops
2 c. lobster (fresh or canned)
1/2 tsp. salt
1 1/2 c. chopped celery
1 c. chopped mushrooms
6 tbsp. butter
1/4 c. flour
1/2 tsp. salt
2 c. milk
1 c. soft bread crumbs
1/4 c. grated cheese

Separate scallops and sprinkle with salt. Cook onions, celery and mushrooms in 2 tbsp. butter until tender. Make a cream sauce with remaining 4 tbsp. butter, flour, salt and milk. Just heat — do not cook. Combine scallops, lobster, vegetables and sauce in 1 1/2 qt. casserole. Top with buttered crumbs, sprinkle with grated cheese. Bake in moderate oven 20 minutes. Serve with steamed rice and tossed salad.

Mussels au Gratin

4 doz. mussels, in shells
4 oz. butter
2 tbsp. flour
1 small onion minced
1/2 c. cheddar cheese, crumbled
2 tbsp. sherry
1 c. cracker crumbs
salt and pepper

Steam cleaned mussels in approximately 1 inch of salted water, for a few minutes just until the shells begin to open. Strain the fluid through a fine sieve and reserve for use later. Remove mussels from shells. Melt 2 oz. butter in a saucepan over medium heat. Add onion and saute until golden brown. Add flour slowly and stir smooth. Slowly stir in 1 c. of the cooking broth; thickened and add sherry; salt and pepper to taste. In a greased casserole alternate layer of mussels, sauce, crumbs and cheese ensuring the top layer is crumbs and cheese. Dot with the remaining butter. Bake at 350⁰F for 15 minutes or until top is browned.

4 servings

Clam Whiffle

1 can clams, drained
12 soda crackers, crumbled
1 c. milk
2 eggs, beaten
1/4 c. butter, melted
2 tbsp. onion, chopped
1 tbsp. green pepper, chopped
1/4 tsp. worcestershire sauce
salt and pepper

Soak cracker crumbs in the milk for a few minutes. Add all remaining ingredients except the eggs. Pour into a greased casserole. Pour eggs over top. Bake at 350⁰F uncovered for 45 minutes.

Curried Lobster

meat from 3 medium size lobsters
1 small onion
1 pt. milk
2 tbsp. butter
2 tbsp. curry powder
2 tbsp. flour mixed with 3 tbsp. milk

Put butter, onion and lobster (cut into medium size pieces) in saucepan. Fry for 5 minutes. Slowly add curry. Stir through. Add milk. Let it heat. Add flour mix. Stir and cook for a little more than 1 minute. Serve with rice.

Codfish the Long Way

2 lbs. salt cod
1 sliced medium turnip
3 medium parsnips (optional)
1/2 lb. pork scraps (or bacon)
2 tbsp. butter
2 qts. cold water
6 mediums carrots, halved
6 medium potatoes
3 large onions sliced

Cut cod in 1" squares. Put in 2 qts. cold water. Simmer for 1 hour. Change water. Put back on stove to simmer. In another pot cook vegetables. About 15 minutes before vegetables are cooked add dumplings (see recipe for dumplings). While dumplings cook fry together onion and pork scraps until lightly browned, add butter to melt. When ready to serve, put dumplings on one platter, vegetables on another. Drain fish, add to vegetables, then pour the onion and pork scraps over the fish.

Halibut in Mushroom Sauce

4 halibut steaks
2 tbsp. butter
1/2 c. mushrooms, sliced
1/2 c. sour cream
2 tbsp. dry sherry
salt
paprika

Sprinkle halibut with salt and place in a greased shallow baking dish. Cook mushrooms in melted butter over medium heat for a couple of minutes. Remove from heat and stir in sour cream and sherry. Spoon mixture over halibut and bake approximately 10 minutes until fish flakes easily.

4 servings

Main Dishes

Photo taken around 1947

Sweet and Sour Pork Chops

4 pork chops, cut 3/4 inch thick
1 tbsp. oil
1/4 c. ketchup
1/2 c. pineapple juice
1 tbsp. brown sugar
2 tbsp. lemon juice
2 tbsp. chopped onion
1 tsp. worcestershire sauce
1/2 tsp. salt
1/8 tsp. ground cloves

Brown chops in oil seasoned with a little salt and pepper. Combine other ingredients and pour over chops. Cover and simmer about 45 minutes or until meat is tender, basting occasionally. Skim excess fat from sauce before serving.

Sweet and Sour Spareribs

Brown spareribs in frying pan until tender. Prepare a sauce with the following ingredients:

2 tbsp. soya sauce
6 tbsp. brown sugar
4 tbsp. vinegar
2 c. water

Mix all the ingredients and cook over medium heat for 10 minutes. Pour over ribs and simmer for 30 minutes. Serve with steamed rice.

Sweet and Sour Pork Chops
Sauce:
Combine
1/2 c. water
1 c. chili sauce
1 onion, chopped
3 tbsp. brown sugar
3 tbsp. vinegar
1 tsp. worcestershire sauce
1 tsp. prepared mustard or 1/2 tsp. dry mustard

Brown sufficient pork chops quickly and drain off fat. Add sauce to chops and bake in a slow oven two or three hours at 250^{0}F.

Pork Tenderloin Dinner
2 tenderloins about 1 lb. each
12 dried prunes
1 tart apple chopped
3/4 c. cold water
2 tbsp. flour
1/4 tsp. salt
1/8 tsp. pepper

Cook prunes in boiling water five minutes. Drain and remove pits. Cut tenderloins lengthwise almost in half. Sprinkle cut sides with salt and pepper. Place 1/2 of prunes and apple down center one side of each tenderloin. Cover with the other side. Fasten with metal skewers and lace with string. Place on rack in shallow roasting pan and cook 1 1/4 hours. Remove pork. Add 3/4 c. water to roasting pan. Stir to loosen brown particles. Pour into saucepan and heat to boiling. Shake 1/4 c. water and 2 tbsp. flour until smooth. Stir into drippings. Heat to boiling, stirring constantly. Add 1/4 tsp. salt and 1/8 tsp. pepper. Boil and stir 1 minute.

Pork Pie

1 lb. ground pork
1/2 lb. ground beef
1 medium onion chopped
1 clove garlic, chopped
1/2 c. water
1 1/2 tsp. salt
1/2 tsp. thyme
1/4 tsp. sage
1/4 tsp. pepper
1/8 tsp. ground cloves

Heat all ingredients to boiling, stirring constantly. Cook, stirring constantly, until meat is light brown but still moist about 5 minutes. Prepare pastry. Preheat oven to 425^{0}F.

Pastry

2/3 c. plus 2 tbsp. shortening
2 c. flour (all-purpose)
1 tsp. salt
1 egg, slightly beaten
2 to 3 tbsp. cold water

Cut shortening into flour and salt until particles are size of peas. Mix egg and water and add to flour mixture to moisten. Divide dough in two for top and bottom. Roll out. Cut slit in top to allow steam to escape. Pour meat into pastry-lined pan and cover with top pastry. Seal edges with fork dipped in flour. (Top layer of pastry should be tucked under bottom layer before sealing). Cover edge with foil until last 15 minutes of baking. Bake 30-40 minutes. Allow to stand 10 minutes before cutting.

Pork Chop Dinner

4 pork chops, 1 inch thick
1/4 c. flour
1/2 tsp. salt
1/4 tsp. pepper
1/4 tsp. paprika
2 tbsp. cooking oil
1 clove garlic
1 c. long grain rice
2 large onions, sliced
1 — 28 oz. can tomatoes
2 tsp. salt
1/4 tsp. pepper
1/2 tsp. dry mustard
1/2 tsp. sweet basil

Combine flour, 1/2 tsp. salt, pepper and paprika. Dip chops in the mixture. Then brown in oil. Add garlic for the last few minutes. Add rice to drippings, cook gently till golden brown. Butter to 13 X 9 1/2 X 2 inch baking dish. Spread rice over bottom of dish. Top with pork chops. Separate onion rings and spread over pork chops. Combine remaining ingredients and pour over chops. Cover tightly. Bake 1 hour covered, then 20-30 minutes uncovered in 350^{0}F until chops are tender.

Turnip Kraut

To prepare the night before:

1 large firm turnip — sliced, peeled and cut french fry style

Put turnip in large glass bowl. Pour approximately 1 c. white vinegar over turnip. Cover with plate and heavy press.

Next day:
Cook corned beef (2-3 lbs.) until almost done. Add turnip and vinegar. Cook until tender. Serve mashed potato on the side. A winter favourite passed down to me.

Serve 4-6 people

Vegetable Medley

6-7 c. mixed cooked vegetables (broccoli, cauliflower, green
   beans, peas, carrots, etc.)
1 can cream of mushroom soup
1 c. shredded sharp cheese
1/3 c. sour cream
1/4 tsp. black pepper
1 jar chopped pimentos (4g)
   or 1 or 2 hot peppers
1 can Durkee french fried onions

Combine cooked vegetables, soup, 1/2 of the cheese, sour
cream, pepper, pimentos and 1/2 of the onions. Pour into
shallow casserole dish (1 qt.). Bake covered at 350°F to heat
through — 15 min. Then remove cover. Crisp top 5 minutes.

Dumplings (for stew, etc.)

2 c. flour
4 tsp. baking powder
1 tsp. salt
2 tsp. butter
1 c. water

Sift dry ingredients. Work in butter with fingers. Add water
and mix. Add to lightly boiling stew or meat or vegetables to
cook in steam. Drop spoonfuls on top of meat or vegetables to
keep out of water. Cover pot tightly and do not remove lid
until done — 15-18 minutes.

Potato-Ham Scallop

1 c. cooked ham, finely diced
4 medium potatoes
2 onions, minced
6 oz. cheddar cheese, grated
4 eggs
1/2 c. light or whipping cream
3 tbsp. butter
1/2 clove garlic, crushed
1 tsp. parsley, minced
1 tsp. chives, minced
3 tbsp. vegetable oil
salt and pepper

Cook onions in oil until tender but not brown. Stir in ham and cook a few minutes longer. Beat eggs and add cream, cheese, garlic and spices. Add ham and onions. Coarsely grate peeled potatoes. Squeeze out their water and stir it into egg mixture. Melt butter in casserole dish and add potato and egg mixture. Place on upper rack of oven and cook at 375°F until top is browned.

4 servings

Cole Cannon

1 small cabbage
4 thin slices of turnip
10 small potatoes
1 large carrot
1 large parsnip
1/2 lb. salt pork

Cut all vegetable in small pieces. Cook turnip, carrots and parsnip until tender. Add potatoes and cook completely. Drain and mash vegetables. Cut salt pork in small pieces and fry until browned. Add to vegetables. Season with salt and pepper.

Chop Suey

1 lb. bean pork
1 — 10 oz. can sliced mushrooms — with liquid
1 — 10 oz. can bean sprouts — with liquid
1/2 c. chopped cabbage
2 tbsp. soya sauce
1 onion chopped
1 1/2 c. chopped celery

Cut pork in small pieces and fry together with the onion. Season with salt and pepper. Add remaining ingredients and cook for 5 minutes. Thicken with a little corn starch.

Sweet and Sour Chicken

1 c. catsup
1 c. barbeque sauce
1/2 c. brown sugar
2 tbsp. flour or cornstarch
1 onion
1/4 c. vinegar

Mix together, pour over chicken. Bake 400-450°F. Cook 35-40 minutes.

Cheese and Rice Casserole

2 c. water
1 c. uncooked rice
1 tsp. salt
1/2 tsp. dry mustard
1/4 tsp. pepper
1 medium onion, chopped
1 medium green pepper, chopped
8 oz. mozzarella cheese, shredded
4 eggs, slightly beaten
2 1/2 c. milk
1/2 c. grated parmesan cheese

Heat water with spices to boiling. Add rice and reduce heat. Cover and simmer for approximately 15 minutes. Remove from heat, stir gently. Let stand covered for another 10 minutes. In a greased baking dish spread 1/2 each of the rice, then onion, then green pepper and finally cheese. Layer the remaining half of the ingredients in the same order. Mix the eggs and milk together and pour over casserole. Top with parmesan cheese. Bake uncovered at 325⁰F for 3/4 hour.

8 servings

Fried Rice with Pork

1 lb. boneless pork
5 slices bacon
2 eggs, beaten
1 c. mushrooms, chopped
1/2 c. green onion, sliced thin
3 c. cooked rice, chilled
1/4 c. soya sauce

Slice pork as thin as possible across the grain in bite-size pieces. Fry bacon crisp in a wok. Drain fat and reserve; crumble bacon on paper toweling. Heat 1 tbsp. bacon fat and cook eggs for about 2 minutes in it. Remove and set aside. Stir fry pork and set aside. Add more bacon drippings and stir fry mushrooms and onion until tender. Shred eggs with a fork. Add all ingredients and cook a couple of minutes. Pour soya sauce over mixture and cook until heated through.

4 servings

Smothered Rabbit

2 rabbits (cut in pieces)
butter or oil
salt and pepper
2 small whole onions
water

In roast pan on top of stove, melt butter and brown rabbit. Season with salt and pepper. Cover rabbit with water, add onion, cover pan and bake in medium oven until tender. Remove rabbit, thicken gravy, put rabbit back in gravy and cook in oven for another 1/2 hour. Serve with potatoes and turnip mashed together or other vegetables.

Livers Paprikash

1 lb. frozen chicken livers
2 tbsp. butter or margarine
1/2 c. chopped celery
1/4 c. chopped onion
cooked noodles or toast
1 — 10 3/4 oz. can condensed cream of mushroom soup
1/2 c. milk or sour cream
1/2 tsp. paprika

In covered skillet, cook livers in butter over low heat until completely thawed — 15 min. Stir occasionally. Uncover; lightly brown livers and cook celery and onion until tender. Blend in soup, milk and paprika. Heat and stir occasionally. Serve over noodles. Makes about 3 cups.

Italian Spaghetti Sauce

3 — 14 oz. cans of tomato sauce
1 lb. hamburg
2 or 3 pork chops
2 or 3 cans mushrooms
3 green peppers
3 hot red peppers
1 c. celery — finely chopped
1 c. cold water
1 tsp. chili powder
1 tsp. oregano
1 tsp. cayenne
1 tsp. Italian seasoning
1 tsp. onion salt
1 tsp. garlic salt
1 tsp. black pepper
10 drops of tabasco sauce
1 tsp. celery salt

Put tomato sauce in pot and add 1 tin of water for each of the 3 cans of sauce. Cook. Mix spices in a measuring cup and add to sauce mixture. Fry beef and pork separately and break into small pieces before adding to the sauce. Simmer for 6 to 7 hours.

Sausage Dressing for Chicken or Turkey

1 lb. sausage meat, hot sausage if available
    (use lb. sausage for each 6 lb. chicken)
large onion
bread crumbs or herb season stuffing
    (if using bread crumb add summer savory)
salt and pepper

Fry sausage meat, cook onions in fat from sausage. If using herb stuffing moisten it with water, mix all together. Fill cavity of chicken or turkey.

Cornish Hens

4 cornish hens

Stuffing:

1/4 c. canned crushed pineapple, drained
1 medium onion, minced
2 tbsp. melted butter
2 c. coarse bread crumbs
2 tsp. summer savory
salt and pepper to taste

Baste:

2 tbsp. honey
1 tsp. soya sauce
1/4 c. pineapple juice

Mix stuffing ingredients and moisten with hot water. Stuff birds and roast at 350^{0}F for approximately 1 hour. Mix baste ingredients in a small saucepan and apply to birds during cooking.

Chicken Casserole

3 c. cooked chicken, chopped
3 c. rice, which was cooked in chicken broth
6 oz. chicken broth
1 can (10 oz.) condensed cream of mushroom soup
2 c. cheddar cheese, grated
2 tbsp. margarine
1 c. onions, chopped
2 c. celery, chopped
1/2 c. mushrooms, sliced
2 oz. pimento, chopped
salt and pepper

Mix soup and chicken broth together. Melt margarine in large skillet over medium heat, add onions and celery and cook until tender, not brown. Add remaining ingredients and mix well. Turn into a greased 12 X 8 baking dish and sprinkle with cheese. Bake at 350°F for 30 minutes.

6 servings

Pasties

Pastry
5 c. flour
1 tbsp. brown sugar
1 tbsp. salt
1/2 tsp. baking powder
1 lb. lard
3/4 c. cold water
1 egg
2 tsp. vinegar

To Brush Over Top
1 egg with 1 tbsp. water
seeds (poppy, caraway or sesame)

Roll dough on lightly floured surface to 1/8" thick. Cut in 4" (diameter) circles. Place circles on ungreased cookie sheet. Spread a scant tbsp. of filling on 1/2 of pastry. Moisten pastry edge with egg mixture and fold over. Seal edge with fork. Brush with egg mixture. Sprinkle with seeds if desired. Bake at 400°F for 15-20 minutes or until golden brown. Serve warm.

Ham Filling
3 c. finely diced cooked ham
2 tbsp. chopped green pepper
2 tbsp. chopped pimento
1 tbsp. minced onion
1 — 10 1/2 oz. can condensed cream of mushroom soup

Combine all ingredients, mixing well.

Beef Filling
Cut stew beef or round steak into small pieces. Brown well. Add onion, finely diced carrots and turnip — cook as a dry stew.

Crustless Quiche

2 tbsp. butter
1 1/2 c. thinly sliced leeks or green onion
2 tbsp. flour
4 slices chopped bacon
4 eggs
2 c. light cream
1/4 tsp. salt, dash pepper and nutmeg
1 c. shredded Swiss cheese
2 tbsp. parmesan cheese

In slightly melted butter cook leeks until soft but not brown. Stir in flour. Spread in bottom of quiche dish. Partially cook bacon in skillet. Drain well and sprinkle over the leeks. Beat eggs; stir in seasonings and cream. Pour over bacon and leeks. Sprinkle parmesan and swiss cheese on top. Bake 40 minutes in 350°F oven. Serve with garlic bread and tossed salad.

4 servings

Bean Casserole

1/2 lb. bacon chopped
1 lb. hamburger
1/2 c. finely chopped onion
1/2 c. ketchup

Fry the above in large skillet; then add:

1/2 c. brown sugar
1 tsp. mustard
2 tsp. vinegar
1 can beans with pork
1 can lima beans drained
1 can kidney beans
salt and pepper to taste

Mix thoroughly and put in casserole. Bake in 350°F oven for 20-30 minutes. (May be done on top of stove, but stir often to prevent sticking.)

Hobo Dinner

1 lb. ground beef
1/4 c. canned milk
salt and pepper
1 small onion or onion salt
4 potatoes
3 or 4 cheese slices
1 can cream of mushroom soup

Press beef in bottom of large casserole. Sprinkle with milk and salt and pepper. Slice potatoes on meat with onion or onion salt. Lay cheese slices on potatoes. Cover with soup. Bake 1 hour in covered casserole at 350⁰F.

Pickled Green Beans and Corned Beef

When green beans are in season, pickle in brine. (Add salt to water until it will float a medium potato. Snip ends from beans and put in brine. Put a plate in bucket to hold the beans under the water.) Beans should be pickled about 2 weeks and can be kept this way to use all winter. Soak portion of green beans to be used in fresh water overnight. Cook corned beef in large pot adding beans for the last 3/4 hour. Cook dumplings on top of meat and beans for last 15 minutes. Serve with mashed potatoes.

Beer Meatballs

1 lb. ground beef
1/2 c. bread crumbs
1 egg
salt and pepper
1 minced onion

Make these ingredients into balls and brown in frying pan. Marinate balls in following sauce for several hours before cooking in the same sauce for about 1 hour at 300ºF, covered with foil. Remove foil to brown for a little time.

1 bottle chili sauce
1 bottle beer
1/2 c. brown sugar
garlic powder
pepper

Hamburg Casserole

1 c. cooked rice
1 large onion
1 lb. ground beef
1 can mushrooms
1 can tomatoes
1 can tomato sauce

Saute chopped onion in a little butter or margarine; add hamburg and brown. Add rice, and rest of ingredients with salt and pepper to taste. Put in buttered baking dish and top with potato chips, chow mein noodles or cornflakes and bake for 30 minutes in 350ºF oven.

Beef Curry

1/2 c. chopped onion
2 tbsp. curry powder
1 tbsp. cooking oil
2 c. cubed cooked beef, about 12 oz.
2 small apples, unpeeled, chopped
3/4 c. water
1/2 c. raisins
1 tsp. instant beef bouillon
1/2 tsp. salt
1/4 c. cold water
1 tbsp. flour

Cook onion and curry powder in hot oil in a large skillet. Stir in beef, apples, 3/4 c. water, raisins, bouillon and salt. Cover and simmer for 10 minutes. Blend 1/4 c. water with flour and add to mixture in skillet. Cook and stir until thickened and bubbly. Season to taste. Serve over cooked rice.

Ham Loaf

1 lb. ground ham (3 1/2 c.)
1/2 lb. ground beef
1/2 lb. ground pork
2 eggs beaten
1 c. quick-cooking oats
3/4 c. tomato juice
1 small onion, chopped fine
1 tsp. salt
1/4 tsp. pepper
4 slices mozzarella cheese cut diagonally into triangles

Mix all ingredients except cheese. Bake in an ungreased loaf pan in 350°F oven until done (one to one and one-quarter hours). Cool for a few minutes. Make slits 1/3 way through loaf and place cheese at regular intervals. Return to oven only long enough to melt cheese.

6-8 servings

Tasty Meat Loaf

Combine:
1 1/2 lbs. ground beef
1/2 c. grated cheddar cheese
1/4 c. rolled oats
2 onions, chopped
2 tbsp. chopped parsley

Mix together and blend in:
1/3 c. catsup
1 egg
1 tsp. salt
1 tsp. worcestershire sauce
1/2 tsp. pepper

Press into 9 X 5 X 3" pan and top with 3 slices bacon. Bake in 350⁰F oven for 1 hour.

Beef Casserole

2 lbs. beef (round steak or boneless stew meat)
1 onion quartered
1 tbsp. onion flakes
4 carrots pared and halved
4 celery stalks quartered
1/4 c. minute tapioca
2 c. fresh mushrooms or 1 tin drained
1 tsp. salt
1/4 tsp. pepper
1 — 28 oz. tomatoes undrained
3/4 c. dry red wine

Trim beef of fat, cut in 2 in. cubes. Brown in a little fat. Add all the rest of the ingredients. Put in a Dutch oven or casserole with a tight fitting cover. Cook for 4 hours in a 300⁰F oven. Do not remove lid during cooking time.

Serves 6

Cakes

Photo taken around 1942

Lemon Sponge Cake

1 c. sugar
1/2 c. sweet milk
1 1/2 c. flour
2 egg whites, beaten stiff
1/2 c. butter
1 tsp. lemon extract
2 tsp. baking powder

Cream together butter and sugar; then add milk, lemon and flour. Stir in last the whites of eggs which have been beaten stiff with baking powder. Bake at 350°F.

Hot Water Sponge Cake

4 eggs, separated
1 1/2 c. white sugar
1/2 c. boiling water
1 tsp. lemon or vanilla extract
1 1/3 c. sifted flour
1/4 tsp. salt
1 tsp. baking powder

Heat oven to 350°F. Beat egg yolks in a small mixing bowl with mixer at high speed for 2 minutes. Add sugar gradually beating constantly. Beat 1 minute longer. Transfer to a larger bowl. Add boiling water, stirring in gently. Beat egg whites stiff and fold in gently after adding dry ingredients. Pour into an ungreased 10" angel food pan. Bake 1 hour or until top springs back when lightly touched. Invert to cool before removing from pan.

Funnel Cake

4 c. milk
4 eggs
1/2 tsp. soda, dissolved in a little water
4 c. sifted flour (see note below before adding)
1/4 tsp. salt — powdered sugar — lard

Mix the above ingredients together, but use only 3 cups of flour to start, then add enough flour from the fourth cup to form a batter that will flow through a funnel into hot lard. The lard should be 1 inch deep at 375⁰F. Control the flow from the funnel with your finger. After that the frying becomes quite an art — you can crisscross, make swirls, make a figure 8 and so on.

Spice Cake

2 c. brown sugar
2 c. water
1 tsp. each cloves, nutmeg and cinnamon
3/4 c. mazola oil
1 lb. seeded raisins

Boil until raisins are soft. Cool and add:

1 beaten egg
1/2 tsp. salt
3 tsp. soda in 1/2 c. warm water
3 c. flour
nuts (optional)

Bake 1-1 1/2 hours in tube pan or 1 hour in ordinary pan at 300⁰F for 1/2 hour, then 350⁰F.

Sultana Cake

1 c. butter
2 c. white sugar
3 eggs
1 c. warm milk
3 1/2 c. flour
1 1/2 tsp. baking powder
1 lb. sultana raisins
8 oz. red and green cherries
1 tsp. vanilla
1 tsp. lemon
1/2 tsp. salt
1 tsp. almond extract

Bake in tube pan at 325⁰F for 2-2 1/2 hours. Cover with foil for approximately first 1/2 hour.

Cranberry Coffee Cake

2 c. sifted flour
3 tsp. baking powder
3/4 tsp. salt
1/2 c. white sugar
5 tbsp. butter
1 egg beaten
1/2 c. milk
2 1/2 c. cranberries

Sift dry ingredients. Cut in butter with a pastry blender until crumbly. Mix egg and milk. Add to the flour mixture, stirring slowly to mix. Then beat until blended well. Spread batter evenly into an 8 X 8 X 2" buttered baking pan. Sprinkle cranberries evenly over the top.

Topping:
Mix 1/4 c. flour with 3/4 c. brown sugar, then cut in 6 tbsp. butter. It should have the consistency of coarse crumbs. Sprinkle over cranberries.

Bake at 375⁰F for 40 to 45 minutes. Cut into squares. Serve warm.

Coconut Pecan Cake

3 c. all purpose flour
2 tsp. baking powder
1/2 tsp. salt
1 c. butter or margarine, softened
1 1/2 c. sugar
3 eggs
1 tsp. vanilla
1/2 c. water
1/4 c. light cream
1/4 c. + 1/2 tsp. maple syrup
1 — 3 1/2 oz. can shredded coconut
1 c. pecans
1/2 tsp. instant coffee
2 c. icing sugar
pecan halves for garnish

Grease and flour a 10" tube pan. Beat butter and sugar until fluffy. Beat in eggs and vanilla. Combine water, cream and 1/4 cup maple syrup. Sir to blend. Sift together the flour, salt and baking powder and add alternately with the liquid ingredients. Fold in coconut and pecans. Spoon into pan. Bake 1 hour or until done in a 350⁰F oven. Cool 10 minutes. Remove from pan.

Icing:
Combine
2 tbsp. + 2 1/2 tsp. hot water
1/2 tsp. maple syrup
instant coffee

Stir until coffee is dissolved. Stir in icing sugar and drizzle over cake.

Light Fruit Cake

1 c. butter
2 c. sugar
2 tsp. almond extract
4 eggs
1 c. brandy and pineapple juice (1/2 c. each)
1 tsp. salt
1 tsp. baking powder
2 2/3 c. flour
2 c. coconut
1 1/2 c. red and green cherries
1 1/2 c. pineapple pieces (candied or chunks)
1/2 c. slivered almonds
2 c. light raisins

Cream butter and sugar. Add extract and eggs. Add 1 c. flour and use the remaining flour to coat the fruit. Add remaining ingredients. Bake at 275°F for 1 1/2 hours or until done.

Old English Light Fruit Cake

1 lb. butter
1 lb. sugar
1 lb. sultana raisins
1 lb. currants
3/4 lb. mixed peel
1/4 lb. cherries
8 eggs
2 lb. flour sifted together with 4 tbsp. baking powder and a
    little salt

Cream butter and sugar. Add eggs one at a time beating well after each addition. Roll fruit with some of the sifted flour. Then add fruit last. Bake 3 hours, very slowly at first.

Yield — 2 medium round cakes

Jelly Roll

3 eggs
1 c. white sugar
1 tsp. lemon extract
1 c. flour
1 tsp. baking powder
1/2 tsp. salt
5 tbsp. hot water

Beat eggs 15 minutes. Add the sugar a little at a time. Add dry ingredients. Add water and flavouring last. Bake 14 minutes at 400°F. Spread with jam or jelly. Roll in damp cloth until set. Reroll in wax paper or foil for storage.

Strawberry Shortcake

2 c. flour, sifted
4 tbsp. baking powder
1/4 tsp. salt
2 tbsp. sugar
6 tbsp. shortening
1 egg, well beaten
1/2 c. milk (approx.)
4 c. sweetened crushed strawberries

Sift all dry ingredients together. Cut in shortening until thoroughly mixed. Combine egg and milk. Add slowly to dry ingredients to form a soft dough. Press dough until it fits in a 8" layer cake pan. Bake in hot oven for 25 to 30 minutes or until lightly browned. Remove from pan while still hot. Split. Butter each half generously. Spread sweetened berries over one layer. Top with the other half of cake. Spoon remaining berries over top. Serve with whipped cream.

Carrot Cake

1 c. sugar
1 c. mazola oil
3 eggs
1/2 tsp. salt
1 1/3 c. flour
1 1/3 tsp. baking powder
1 1/3 tsp. soda
1 1/3 tsp. cinnamon
2 c. grated raw carrots
1/2 c. chopped nuts

Icing

4 oz. cream cheese
1/4 c. butter
grated rind from 1 orange
vanilla
2 c. icing sugar

Mix in order given. Bake in 350°F oven for 30 minutes.

Chocolate Cake

1 1/2 c. brown sugar
1/2 c. butter or shortening
2 eggs
3/4 c. sour milk
3 squares chocolate
2 c. flour
1 tsp. soda dissolved in the sour milk
1/2 c. boiling water — added last

Cream sugar and butter well. Add eggs. Add chocolate which has been melted. Add the sour milk — soda mixture. Add flour and lastly boiling water. Bake at 350°F for 30 minutes.

Dratcher's Chocolate Christmas Cake

In Large Bowl:
1/2 c. butter
2 c. sugar
8 squares semi-sweet chocolate

In Medium Bowl:
2 c. flour
1/2 tsp. salt
2 tsp. baking powder

In Small Bowl:
4 eggs (beaten)
2 tsp. vanilla extract
1 tsp. almond extract
1/2 c. milk or wine or coffee or grape juice or brandy
1 tsp. lemon extract

On Flat Tray — With Handful of Flour:
1 c. chopped nuts (coconut, walnuts)
1 c. chopped fruit (figs, dates, cherries)

Mix small bowl into large bowl, then alternately mix medium bowl and flat tray ingredients into the large bowl. Grease pan, put wax paper in, grease paper, put more wax paper in, grease again (use tube pan). Bake 1/2 hour at 300⁰F — then 1 1/2 hours at lower heat — 250⁰F. Store in a cool place for one month.

Coconut Pound Cake

1 1/2 c. margarine
3 c. cake flour, sifted
3 c. sugar
5 eggs
7 oz. coconut
1/2 c. evaporated milk diluted with 1/2 c. water
1 tsp. salt
2 tsp. vanilla
2 tsp. almond or coconut extract

Cream butter and sugar. Add eggs one at a time. Sift flour then measure. Add salt and sift again. Add flour alternately with milk. Add flavourings. Fold in coconut. Bake in a greased and floured 10 inch tube pan at 325^0F for 1 1/2 hours.

Cheese Cake

1 pkg. lemon jello
3 tbsp. lemon juice
1 c. boiling water
3 c. graham wafer crumbs
1/2 c. melted butter
1 pkg. (8 oz.) Philadelphia Cream Cheese
1 c. sugar
1 tsp. vanilla
1 tin evaporated milk

In a small bowl dissolve jello in boiling water. Add lemon juice. Set aside to cool. Add melted butter to graham crumbs. Pat in bottom of glass 9" X 13" pan, lightly buttered. Bake 375^0F for about 8 minutes or until golden. Cool. Cream cheese, sugar and vanilla. Add cooled jello. Mix well. In a large bowl, whip milk until firm. Fold gelatine mixture into milk. Pour into cooled graham crumbs. Chill for several hours. Top with your favourite topping. (cherry, strawberry, blueberry . . .)

No Cheese Cheesecake

4 eggs separated
1 can sweetened condensed milk
1/3 c. lemon juice
1 tsp. grated lemon rind
1 tsp. vanilla extract
2/3 c. graham wafer crumbs
2 tbsp. melted butter or margarine

In large bowl, beat egg yolks. Add condensed milk and blend well. Add lemon juice, rind and vanilla and blend well. In a separate bowl beat egg whites until stiff but not dry. Fold into milk mixture. Combine crumbs with butter or margarine. Mix well. Spread all but a few spoonfuls evenly over the bottom of a buttered 9 inch square pan. Pour in filling mixture and sprinkle the remaining crumb mixture over the top. Bake at 325^{0}F for 30 minutes. Cool 1 hour in oven with the door closed.

Almost As Good As Poundcake

1 c. butter
1 2/3 c. sugar
5 eggs
2 c. flour
2 1/2 tsp. lemon
1/4 to 1/2 c. milk (if needed)

Beat butter until creamy; gradually add sugar. Beat eggs in one at a time. Add flour and lemon. Add milk as required. Bake at 300^{0}F for 1 hour or until done.

Creamy Rich Cheesecake

1/2 c. margarine
2 c. graham wafer crumbs
1/4 c. icing sugar
3 — 250g pkg. cream cheese
3 eggs
1/2 c. sugar (use more or less according to taste)
2 tsp. vanilla
1 can cherry pie filling or homemade fruit topping

Preheat oven to 350°F. Melt margarine and add to crumbs in a small bowl, mix well and then add icing sugar. Press mixture into large pie plate. Beat until fluffy in a large bowl the cream cheese. Add sugar, eggs, vanilla, beat well until all ingredients are combined. Pour mixture in the pie plate, on top of the crust. Bake in the preheated oven for 30 minutes or until the cake doesn't jiggle. When the cake is completely cooled, pour pie filling over the cheesecake. Cut and serve.

Desserts

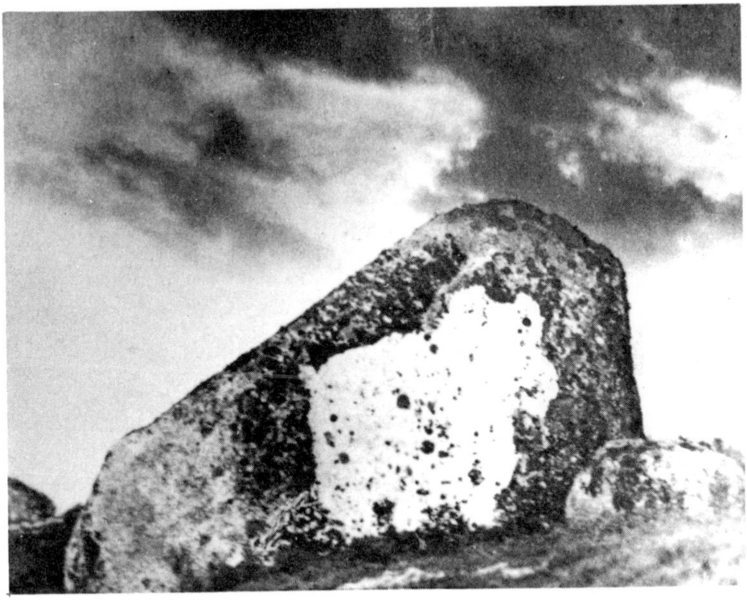

Image of bear

Granola Bars
(A nutritious snack for the whole family)

3 c. rolled oats
1 c. peanuts, chopped
1 c. raisins
1 c. chocolate chips (optional)
1 can sweetened condensed milk
1/2 c. melted butter

Preheat oven to 325^{0}F. Line 15 X 10" pan with foil; grease. In large mixing bowl, combine all ingredients; mix well. Press evenly into prepared pan. Bake 25 to 30 minutes or until golden brown. Cool slightly; remove from pan and peel off foil. Cut into bars. Store, loosely covered, at room temperature. Makes 36 bars.

Cocoa-Raisin Clusters
2 c. sugar
1/2 c. butter or margarine
1/2 c. cocoa
1/8 tsp. salt
1/2 c. milk
1 c. raisins
1/2 c. hot water
3 c. rolled oats
1/2 c. peanut butter
1 tsp. vanilla

In a large saucepan, combine sugar, butter, cocoa, salt and milk. Bring to a full boil over medium heat, stirring constantly. Let boil 1 minute. Meanwhile, in a small bowl, soak raisins in hot water 1-2 minutes. Remove cocoa mixture from heat and add remaining ingredients. Stir until well blended. Drop mixture by teaspoonfuls onto wax paper. Chill until set.

2 1/2 dozen candies

Rum Balls

1 c. crushed vanilla wafers
1 c. confectioners sugar
1 1/2 c. chopped pecans
2 tbsp. cocoa
2 tbsp. light corn syrup (or honey)
4 tbsp. rum
1/2 c. granulated sugar

Mix together all dry ingredients. Add syrup and rum. Mix well. Shape into balls about 3/4" in diametre and roll in granulated sugar. Store in air-tight containers. (These freeze well.)

Maids of Honour

Rub together:
3/4 c. sugar
3/4 c. butter

Add:
1 egg, well beaten
grated rind of one lemon

Add:
1 tbsp. milk
1 1/2 c. flour

Mix together and shape into balls. Put into small muffin tins and make hole in center and fill with jam. Bake at 350°F until brown.

Family Dessert

1 can evaporated milk
1 pkg. lemon jello
salt
2 lemons
1 1/2 c. boiling water
1/2 c. sugar
1 pkg. graham wafers

Place milk in cube tray until it starts to thicken — not hard.
Dissolve jello with 1 1/2 cups boiling water. Place in fridge
until it begins to thicken. Make crust from graham wafers or
vanilla wafers with 1/2 c. soft margarine. Pour milk in large
bowl and beat until very light. Add sugar, salt, lemon juice and
rind. Add jello and beat. Pour mixture over crumbs. Save a
few crumbs to sprinkle over top.

Mum's Gingerbread

Mix together:
1 egg
1/2 c. sugar
1/2 c. shortening
1 c. molasses

Mix and add to above:
2 1/2 c. flour
2 tsp. soda
1/2 tsp. salt
1/2 tsp. cloves
1 tsp. each cinnamon, ginger, mixed spice and allspice

Then add 1 cup boiling water and mix well. Line a 9 X 13 or 9
X 9 pan with greased wax paper and spread batter. Bake in a
moderate oven for 45 to 50 minutes.

Plum Pudding

1 1/4 c. flour
1/2 tsp. each cinnamon and nutmeg
1/4 tsp. each mace and cloves
1/3 tsp. salt
1 1/2 c. bread crumbs
1 1/2 c. shredded suet
1 1/2 c. brown sugar
1 c. sultana raisins
1 c. seeded raisins
1 c. currants
1 c. chopped figs
1 1/2 c. mixed peel
3/4 c. blanched almonds, sliced
1 1/2 c. glaced cherries, halved
1/2 c. honey
4 eggs, well beaten
1/2 c. wine or brandy
1/2 to 2/3 c. milk
1/2 tsp. baking soda, dissolved in
1 tbsp. warm water

(The amount of milk will depend on the staleness of crumbs.)
Mix ingredients in order given. Fill well-buttered moulds or
bowls 2/3 full. Cover with strong paper. Tie down with
pudding cloth and steam 5 hours.

Fruit Jelly Dessert

2 pkg. raspberry or strawberry jello
1 pkg. frozen raspberries or strawberries
1 carton sour cream
1 c. crushed pineapple
2 bananas, mashed

Bring juices from frozen berries and pineapple to a boil.
Dissolve jello in hot juice. Add fruit. Pour one-half into mold
and let chill until partially set. Add sour cream to mixture in
mold. Put remainder of jelly mixture on top. Set overnight.
Unmold and top with whipped topping.

Brownies

2 squares unsweetened chocolate
1/3 c. butter
2/3 c. all purpose flour
1/2 tsp. baking powder
1/4 tsp. salt
2 eggs
1 c. sugar
1 tsp. vanilla
1/2 c. chopped nuts

Melt chocolate with butter over hot water. Cool. Sift flour with baking powder and salt. Beat eggs and gradually add sugar. Continue beating until well blended. Blend in chocolate mixture and vanilla. Stir in flour mixture and nuts. Spread in a greased and floured 8 inch square pan. Bake at 350°F for 25 to 30 minutes.

Date Squares

2 c. flour
3/4 tsp. baking soda
1 tsp. baking powder
1 tsp. salt
1 c. butter
1 c. brown sugar
2 c. oatmeal

1/2 lb. chopped dates
1/2 c. cold water
2 tbsp. brown sugar
piece of butter, the size of an egg

Sift flour, baking powder, soda and salt. Rub in butter with tips of fingers. Add sugar and oatmeal, mix well. Spread half the crumbs in a greased shallow pan 8 X 14. Pat to smoothen. Cook last four ingredients and cool. Spread over crumb mixture in pan and top with the other half of crumbs. Pat to smooth. Bake at 325°F for about 30 minutes.

Peanut Butter Squares

1 c. flour
1 tbsp. brown sugar
6 tbsp. butter
pinch salt

Mix together; spread in 8 X 8" pan. Bake 10 minutes.

1 c. brown sugar
1 c. chopped nuts
1 c. coconut
1 tbsp. flour
1/2 tsp. baking powder
1/3 tsp. salt
2 eggs

Mix above ingredients and spread over first mixture. Return
to oven for 30 minutes. When cool, ice with the following:

1 c. icing sugar
pinch salt
1 tbsp. butter
2 tbsp. peanut butter
2 to 3 tbsp. hot water

To sugar and salt, add butter and peanut butter. Add hot
water and beat thoroughly.

Blackberry Almond Bars

A treat to look at! Even better to eat!

1 1/2 c. all-purpose flour
1/2 c. brown sugar
1/4 c. granulated sugar
1/2 tsp. baking powder
1/2 tsp. salt
1/2 tsp. cinnamon
1/2 c. butter or margarine
1 egg
1 tsp. almond extract
2 tbsp. flour
3/4 c. blackberry jam (or your choice)
1 egg yolk
1 tsp. water

Combine flour, both sugars, baking powder, salt and cinnamon. Mix well. Cut in butter until mixture resembles coarse meal. Beat egg and almond extract with a fork and add to first mixture. Remove 1/2 cup of mixture and add the 2 tablespoons of flour to it and set aside. Press remaining mixture in 9 X 9" pan, lightly greased. Spread jam evenly. Add enough water to reserved mixture until it holds together. Roll out and cut into 12 strips. Weave strips over jam to form a lattice. Brush with mixture of egg yolk and 1 tsp. water. Bake at 375^{0}F for 25-30 minutes, until golden. Cool and cut into bars.

Coconut Bars

1/2 c. firmly packed brown sugar
1 c. flour
1/2 c. melted butter
1 c. firmly packed brown sugar
2 tbsp. flour
1 tsp. baking powder
1/2 tsp. salt
1 c. shredded coconut
1 1/2 c. rice krispies
1 tsp. vanilla
2 eggs

(1) Combine 1/2 c. brown sugar and 1 c. flour with melted butter. Stir well and press mixture into ungreased pan. Set aside. (2) Combine next six ingredients and set aside. (3) Beat eggs until frothy; mix in vanilla. Fold in dry ingredients and spread over prepared base in pan. Bake in 350°F oven for 15-20 minutes or until golden brown. Cool and cut into bars.

Cherry Squares

6 tbsp. cocoa
1/2 c. butter
1/2 c. brown sugar
1 c. flour

Press in pan and bake for 10 minutes.

2 eggs
1 c. brown sugar
1/2 tsp. baking powder
2 tbsp. flour
1/2 c. walnuts
1/2 c. split cherries
1 c. coconut
1 tsp. vanilla
dash salt

Mix and spread.

Cracker Squares

30 salted crackers, rolled fine
1 c. brown sugar
1 1/2 tsp. baking powder
3 tbsp. flour
1 c. coconut
1/4 c. cherries
1 egg in a measuring cup, fill with milk

Mix all ingredients and smoothen in a 8 X 8 greased pan. Bake at 350⁰F for 30 minutes. Frost with lemon flavoured butter icing.

Butterscotch Sticks

1/4 c. butter
1 c. brown sugar
1/4 c. nuts
1 tsp. baking powder
1/4 tsp. salt
1 c. sifted flour
1 egg
1 tsp. vanilla

Melt butter in saucepan, add sugar and when well blended remove from heat and cool to lukewarm. Add unbeaten egg to mixture and blend well. Sift flour, salt and baking powder and add to sugar mixture. Add vanilla. Spread in greased 8 X 8" pan and sprinkle nuts on top. Bake 30 minutes in 375⁰F oven.

Walnut Snacks

1/3 c. butter
1/3 c. brown sugar
2 egg yolks
1 tsp. vanilla
1 1/2 c. flour
1 tsp. baking powder
salt

Cream butter, sugar, egg yolks and vanilla. Beat well. Sift flour. Add salt, baking powder. Mix together — put in pan.

Spread:
2 egg whites, well beaten
1 c. brown sugar
1 c. walnuts

Bake 20 minutes at 350⁰F in greased pan.

Jam Squares

1 c. flour, sifted
1 tsp. baking powder
1/2 c. butter
1 egg beaten
1 tbsp. milk
pinch of salt

Rub butter and flour together which has been sifted with salt and baking powder. Add beaten egg and milk. Spread in pan and cover with strawberry or raspberry jam.

1 egg beaten
1 c. sugar
2 c. coconut
small piece of butter
1 tsp. vanilla

Mix together, spread over jam. Bake at 350⁰F for 30 to 45 minutes until a light brown. Cut into squares when cooled.

Chocolate Bar Squares

(Bottom)
1/2 c. soft butter
1/4 c. sugar
5 tbsp. cocoa
1 egg, lightly beaten
1 tsp. vanilla
2 c. fine graham — wafer crumbs
1 c. coconut
1/2 c. chopped nuts

(Centre)
1/4 c. butter
1/4 c. milk (carnation)
2 tbsp. instant banana pudding mix (or your choice)
2 c. icing sugar
1/4 tsp. salt
1/2 tsp. vanilla (optional, depending on pudding mix)

(Top)
4 squares baker's chocolate
1 tbsp. butter
1/4 tsp. vanilla

Step 1:
Combine butter, sugar, cocoa and egg in top of double boiler. Set over simmering water and cook stirring constantly until thick and smooth, about 5 minutes. Stir in vanilla.

Step 2:
Combine graham crumbs, coconut and nuts in bowl. Stir into first mixture.

Step 3:
Spoon mixture into buttered 9 inch square glass pan and pack down firmly. Spread with filling. Chill for 15 minutes.

Step 4:
Combine chocolate and butter in top of double boiler and set over simmering water until melted. Stir in vanilla and spread over the top of other layers while hot. Chill. Cut in small squares. Refrigerate.

Butterscotch Chipet Squares

In a double boiler, melt:
1 pkg. butterscotch chips
1/4 c. margarine
1/2 c. peanut butter

Cool and add:
1 c. coconut
1 pkg. colored minature marshmallows

Pat in a 8 X 8 pan. Frost with butter icing.

Pineapple Graham Wafer Squares

2 1/2 c. graham wafer crumbs
1/2 c. melted butter
1 1/2 c. icing sugar
2 eggs
1 can crushed pineapple, drained
1/2 c. butter, creamed
1/2 pint cream, whipped

Mix 2 1/4 c. graham wafer crumbs with 1/2 c. melted butter. Press in a well greased 9 X 9 inch pan. Bake 15 minutes at 325°F. Allow to cool. Cream 1/4 c. butter, gradually blend in 1 1/2 c. sifted icing sugar. Add 2 unbeaten eggs. Beat until very light. Spread evenly over the first mixture. Fold drained pineapple into whipped cream. Spread over mixture. Top with 1/4 c. wafer crumbs. Chill in refrigerator for a few hours. Cut in squares.

Double Chocolate Crumble Bars

Cream:
1/2 c. margarine
3/4 c. sugar

Add:
2 eggs

Stir in the following:
3/4 c. flour
2 tbsp. cocoa
1/4 tsp. baking powder

Put in buttered 8 X 8" pan and bake 15 to 20 minutes at 350⁰F. Cover with 2 cups minimallows. Put in oven to melt. Cool. While the above cools, combine 1 small pkg. chipits and 1 cup peanut butter and melt over low heat. When melted, remove from heat and stir in 1 1/2 c. rice krispies and spread over the base.

Trifle

2 pkg. jello
custard powder (Birds)
1 pt. whipping cream
5 types of fruit
1/2 c. sherry (or more)
sponge cake

The Day Before:
In large glass trifle dish arrange a 2-3" layer of cake or pkg. of lady finger biscuits in bottom. Pour sherry evenly over cake. Layer fruit (eg. pineapple). Dissolve 1 jello with hot water and ice for quicker setting. Pour partially set jello over cake, let set overnight.

Next Day:
Arrange a layer of fruit on jelly (eg. canned mandarin oranges). Dissolve 2nd jello. Pour partially set jello over fruit. Let set. Arrange a layer of fruit in jello (eg. raspberries). Prepare custard (directions on tin). Allow to cool to room temperature. Then pour over fruit. Let set. Then a layer of fruit (eg. banana). Cover with whipped cream, topped with sliced kiwi fruit and strawberries (or other decorative topping — eg. cherries, chocolate chips, cake decorations). Remember to emphasize layers — choose contrasting colours of jello and fruit. The better it looks the better it tastes.

Cranberry Nut Pie

1 1/2 c. cranberries
1/2 c. seeded raisins
1/2 c. chopped walnuts
1 tbsp. butter
2 tbsp. flour
1/4 c. orange juice

Mix all the above ingredients and allow to stand while mixing and rolling your favourite pastry. Line 9 inch pie plate and fill with the fruit mixture. Cover with pastry strips, lattice-fashion and bake in 400°F oven for 10 minutes and reduce heat to 350°F for another 30 or 35 minutes.

Strawberry Pie

1 qt. fresh strawberries
1/2 c. water
1 tsp. lemon juice
1/2 c. sugar
1 pkg. strawberry jello
1 baked pie shell

Blend 1 cup strawberries; add water and lemon juice. Blend until smooth. Place in saucepan, add sugar and jello. Heat to boiling point and boil for 2 minutes stirring constantly. Remove from heat and cool slightly. While glaze is cooling, arrange remaining strawberries cut in half in baked shell with cut side down. Pour warm glaze over berries and refrigerate for 3 hours. Serve with whipped cream.

Pecan Pie

1/2 c. white sugar
1 tbsp. flour
2 tbsp. milk
2 eggs, beaten
1 c. chopped pecans
1 c. brown sugar, not firmly packed
1 tsp. vanilla
1/4 c. margarine or butter
1 — 9 inch unbaked pie shell

Mix all ingredients except butter and pecans and mix well. Melt butter and add. Fold in pecans. Pour into unbaked pie shell and bake at 350°F for 30 to 35 minutes.

Shortbread Cookies

1/2 c. corn starch
1/2 c. icing sugar
1 c. flour, sifted
3/4 c. butter

Sift dry ingredients together. Blend in butter with a spoon, mixing until soft smooth dough forms. Shape dough in 1 inch balls. Flatten with a fork. Bake at 330°F 20 to 25 minutes.

Bachelor's Buttons

1 c. butter
3/4 c. brown sugar
1/4 tsp. salt
1 egg
2 c. flour
2 tsp. baking powder
vanilla

Cream butter and sugar and add well-beaten egg. Add sifted flour, salt and baking powder. Roll out dough on a floured board. Cut into round cookies. Cover one cookie with jelly and put another cookie on top. Bake at 350°F until brown.

Christmas Icebox Cookies

1 c. soft butter
3/4 c. brown sugar
1/2 tsp. vanilla
1/8 tsp. salt
2 1/2 c. sifted flour
1 c. almonds sliced lengthwise or walnuts
1/2 c. each red and green whole cherries

Cream butter. Add sugar and then add vanilla, salt and flour. Finally add nuts and cherries and form into rolls. Store in refrigerator overnight. Slice thinly with a sharp knife. Bake on greased baking sheet in 375°F oven for 10 minutes.

Swedish Ginger Cookies

1 c. butter
1 1/2 c. sugar
1 egg
1 1/2 tbsp. grated orange peel
2 tbsp. dark corn syrup
1 tbsp. water
3 1/4 c. flour
2 tbsp. soda
2 tsp. cinnamon
1 tsp. ginger
1/2 tsp. cloves

Chill dough. Roll thin. Bake in a hot oven.

Shortbread Sparkles

1 c. butter or margarine
1/2 c. white sugar
1/3 c. brown sugar
1 egg
1 tsp. lemon rind
2 1/2 c. all purpose flour

Cream together first 3 items. Add the egg and mix well. Add rind and flour. Bake at 375°F for 8 to 10 minutes. Decorate.

Ice Box Cookies

1 c. butter
1/2 c. brown sugar
1 c. white sugar
2 eggs, unbeaten
3 1/2 c. flour
1/2 tsp. salt
1 tsp. baking soda
1/2 tsp. baking powder
1 tsp. vanilla
1 c. walnuts

Sift all dry ingredients together. Then mix ingredients as listed together. Line a loaf pan with wax paper. Put dough in pan and store in the freezer over night. Remove from pan and slice dough thin. Bake at 325⁰F.

Soft Molasses Cookies

3/4 c. shortening
1 c. brown sugar
1 egg
1 c. molasses
4 scant c. flour
1 tsp. ginger
1 tsp. cinnamon
1 tsp. cloves
1 tsp. soda
1 tsp. baking powder
1 tsp. salt
1 tsp. cream of tartar
1 tsp. nutmeg
1 c. milk

Sift all dry ingredients together. Mix alternately with milk to creamed well blended mixture of the first 4 items. Roll out quite thick. Bake at 400⁰F.

Raisin-Filled Chocolate Chip Cookies

1 c. (2 sticks) margarine, softened
3/4 c. firmly packed light brown sugar
3/4 c. granulated sugar
1 tsp. vanilla
1 tsp. water
2 eggs
2 1/4 c. sifted all purpose flour
1 tsp. baking soda
1/2 tsp. salt
2 c. raisins
12 oz. semisweet chocolate pieces

Beat softened margarine, brown and white sugars, vanilla, water and eggs in a large bowl until creamy and thoroughly blended. Stir in flour, baking soda and salt by hand. Mix well. Stir in raisins and chocolate pieces. Drop dough by teaspoonful on an ungreased cookie sheet allowing 1 1/2 to 2 inches between cookies for spreading. Bake in a preheated oven 375⁰F for 8 minutes of until cookies are nicely browned, depending on how crisp or well done you like them.

Chocolate Chip Cookies

1/2 c. shortening
1/4 c. white sugar
1/2 c. brown sugar
1 egg
1 tsp. vanilla
1 c. flour
1/2 tsp. baking soda
1/2 tsp. salt
1 c. chocolate chips
1/2 c. slivered almonds (optional)

Cream shortening, brown sugar, white sugar and vanilla. Beat in egg. Combine flour, baking soda and salt. Add to creamed mixture slowly. Stir in chocolate chips and almonds. Bake at 375⁰F for 10-12 minutes.

Molasses Cookies

2 1/4 c. flour
2 level tsp. baking soda
1/2 c. warm water (not hot)
1 tsp. cinnamon
1/2 c. shortening
1 egg, beaten
1/2 c. molasses
1 tsp. ginger
1/4 tsp. salt
1/2 c. sugar

Cream shortening and sugar until light and fluffy. Add unbeaten egg and molasses and beat well. Sift all dry ingredients together and add alternately to the creamed mixture with the water a little at a time. When adding the flour cut in a few raisins if desired. Drop by small teaspoonfuls on an ungreased baking pan. Sprinkle with sugar. Bake at 375°F for 15 to 20 minutes.

Approximately 2 dozen cookies

Perfect Raisin Drops

Boil briskly for 5 minutes 2 cups raisins (or dates) and 1 cup water. Then stir in 1 tsp. soda and set aside to cool.

Mix the following:
1 c. shortening
2 c. brown sugar
3 well beaten eggs
3 c. plus 3 tbsp. flour
1/2 tsp. salt
1 tsp. baking powder
1/4 tsp. nutmeg
1 tsp. cinnamon
1 tsp. vanilla
nuts if desired

Stir in first mixture. Drop by spoonful on a greased baking sheet. Bake in moderate oven.

Miscellaneous

Cheese Ball

8 oz. cream cheese
4 oz. blue cheese, crumbled
4 oz. sharp cheddar, shredded
1/4 c. minced onion
1 tbsp. worcestershire sauce
finely snipped parsley

Place cheese in small mixer bowl and let stand at room temperature until softened. Add onion and worcestershire sauce; blend on low speed. Beat on medium speed until fluffy, scraping side and bottom of bowl. Cover and chill at least 8 hours. Shape mixture into 1 large ball or 30-36 1" balls. Roll in parsley and place on serving plate. Cover; chill 2 hours or until firm.

Solomon Gundy

This recipe takes three to five hours to prepare. Soak 12 to 20 salt herring overnight in cold water. Clean herring by scraping and removing skin, back bone and large bones. Cut in approximately two inch pieces. To every cup of white vinegar add 1 tbsp. white sugar and add a few peppercorns. Bring to a full boil; then let cool. In medium size mason jars, put alternate layers of herring and onion rings. Cover with cooled vinegar solution and seal. Refrigerate and leave for at least a week before eating.

Makes 4-6 bottles

Nuts & Bolts

4-21-88
Chapel Belles

1 — 300g cherrios   *10 oz*
1 — 250g shreddies   *7½ oz*
1 — 300g straight pretzel sticks   *10 oz*
2 1/2 lb. salted peanuts
1 1/2 tbsp. celery salt
1 1/2 tbsp. onion salt
2 lb. margarine
1 1/2 tbsp. worcestershire sauce

Cook for about 1 hour at 250ºF stirring occasionally to get the liquid over everything.

Chip or Vegetable Dip

1 1/2 c. sour cream
1 c. mayonnaise
2 tsp. dill weed
1 tsp. lemon juice
1 tsp. celery salt
1 tsp. curry powder
a sprinkle of garlic powder

Combine all ingredients well. Chill. Serve in a bowl with a platter of raw vegetables or chips.

Cucumber Sauce

1/4 c. shortening
2 tbsp. flour
2 c. milk
3 egg yolks, slightly beaten
1 medium cucumber, pared seeded and diced
4 1/2 oz. can shrimp coarsely chopped (1 cup)
1 tsp. salt
1/4 tsp. nutmeg
1/8 tsp. pepper

Melt shortening in saucepan. Add flour and cook over low heat. Remove and add milk. Heat to boiling, stirring constantly. Continue for one minute longer and remove from heat. Stir 1/2 hot mixture into egg yolks. Blend this into remaining hot mixture. Boil and stir one minute. Add remaining ingredients. Heat thoroughly. Serve warm.

Yield — 3 cups

Rosy Apple Jelly

2 c. canned or bottled apple juice
juice of 1 lemon
1/4 tsp. food colouring
1/2 bottle certo
3 c. sugar

Combine juices and colour mixture in a kettle with sugar and stir well. Bring to a full boil, stirring constantly. Boil hard 4 minutes. Add certo. Remove from heat. Skim and pour into hot sterilized jars. Cover with melted parafin wax.

Cherried Cranberries

4 c. fresh or frozen cranberries
2 c. sugar
1/4 tsp. salt
1/4 tsp. baking soda
1 c. boiling water

Put all ingredients in heavy 4 qt. saucepan. Bring to a boil over medium heat, cover and simmer gently for 15 minutes. Do not uncover while cooking. Cool covered. Put in jars with tight lids and store in refrigerator.

Mother's Mustard Pickle

2 qts. green tomatoes
1 qt. pickling onions
1 cauliflower
2 large green pepper

Chop vegetables (leave onions whole unless too large). Cover with cold water and a teacup of pickling salt. Leave overnight. In morning, boil 1/2 hour and drain well.

Sauce:

Boil 2 qts. vinegar. Mix 3/4 flour, 2 cups sugar, 1 cup Keen's mustard. Mix to a smooth paste with water and stir into hot vinegar. Stir constantly until thickened. Cook a few minutes longer. Then add 2 tbsp. tumeric. Cook a few minutes and then add to drained vegetables. Heat thoroughly and bottle.

Hot Pickled Vegies

1 1/2 c. cauliflowerets
3 stalks celery cut in julienne strips
2 medium carrots cut diagonally in thin slices
1 c. brocolli flowerets
4 oz. green beans
1/4 c. green pepper slices
1 c. pearl onions
2 c. cider vinegar
2 c. water
1/2 c. coarse salt
2 tbsp. peppercorns
3/4 tsp. ground cloves

Mix all ingredients in large glass container. Cover and refrigerate at least 48 hours. Store no longer than 2 weeks. Makes 10 cups.

Quince Relish

8 quince peeled and quartered
32 whole cloves
6 c. sugar
2 c. vinegar
2 oranges, sliced and pitted
1 firm apple

Put 2 cloves in each quarter of quince. Cook quince and apple in enough water to cover until soft. Drain and save water. Combine orange, sugar, vinegar and 1 1/3 cups quince water and boil 10 minutes. Add quince and apple and boil 30 minutes. Serve with cold meats. It is also good with toast and tea biscuits.

Bean Relish

4 qt. green or wax beans
6 tsp. flour
1/3 c. dry mustard
1 1/2 tsp. powdered tumeric
1 tsp. celery seed
1/8 tsp. dry curry powder
1 tsp. salt
3 c. cider vinegar
3 c. brown sugar

Wash and tip beans; cut in 1 1/2 inch pieces; there should be 4 qt. after cutting. Cook in boiling salted water until tender. Make a paste of flour, mustard, tumeric, celery seed, curry powder, salt and 1 c. of vinegar. Mix remainder of vinegar and brown sugar in preserving kettle; heat to boiling. Slowly stir in spice paste; cook and stir till smooth and thick. Add drained beans to hot sauce; cook gently for 10 minutes. Remove from heat and seal in sterile jars.

Approximately 8 pint jars

Millionaire Pickles

Cut following into 1 inch pieces:
12-14 cukes (peeled and quartered, remove seeds, cut into 1 inch pieces)
8 large onions
3 red peppers (sweet)
3 green peppers

Cover with 1/2 c. salt and let stand 3 hours. Drain, then add:

1 qt. vinegar
7 c. white sugar
1/4 c. mustard seed
2 tbsp. celery seed
3 tsp. tumeric
8 cloves

Boil all together for 30-40 minutes. Bottle.

Red Chow

12 pears, chopped
13 ripe tomatoes, chopped
6 onions, chopped
2 red or green peppers, chopped
4 c. sugar
4 tbsp. salt
1 qt. vinegar
1/2 pkg. pickling spice (put in cheesecloth bag)

Combine above in large pot. Bring just to a boil and simmer for 1 1/2 to 2 hours stirring frequently to prevent burning. Pour in hot jars and cover with melted parafin wax.

Jello Pudding Fudge

4 oz. pkg. jello pudding, flavour as desired
2 tbsp. butter
1/4 c. milk
1 1/2 c. icing sugar
1/4 c. chopped nuts

Combine pudding mix, butter and milk. Bring to a full boil for 1 minute, stirring constantly. Remove from heat. Quickly stir in sugar and add nuts. Put in a 8 X 4 inch pan.

Magic Chocolate Fudge

1 pkg. semi-sweet chocolate chips
1 can sweetened condensed milk
1 1/4 c. icing sugar
1 tsp. vanilla
1 c. pecans or walnuts, chopped (optional)
pinch of salt

Melt chocolate in top of double boiler over water, stirring occasionally. Remove from heat and stir in the remaining ingredients. Spread mixture evenly in a 8 X 8" wax paper lined pan. Chill until firm. Turn fudge onto a cutting board, remove wax paper and cut in serving squares. Butterscotch chipits may be substituted for the chocolate chips if desired.

Low Calorie Fudge

4 c. white sugar
1 c. evaporated milk
1 tsp. salt
1/2 lb. butter

Boil gently for 10 minutes. Remove from heat and add 1 tsp. vanilla and 2 c. flour. For **Chocolate Fudge** add 5 tbsp. cocoa. For **Peanut Butter Fudge** add 1/2 c. peanut butter.

5 Minute Holiday Fudge

2/3 c. undiluted evaporated milk
1 2/3 c. brown sugar
1/2 tsp. salt

Combine ingredients in saucepan over medium heat. Heat to boiling and cook 5 minutes stirring constantly. Remove from heat and add:

1 1/2 c. diced marshmallows (approx. 16 medium)
1 1/2 c. chocolate chips
1 tsp. vanilla
1/2 c. chopped nuts

Stir until marshmallows melt. Pour into a buttered 9 inch square pan. Allow to cool and cut into squares

Five Minute Fudge

Combine 2/3 c. undiluted evaporated milk with 1 2/3 c. sugar in saucepan. Heat to boiling. Boil five minutes — stirring constantly. Remove from heat and add 1 c. (4 oz.) mini marshmallows, 1/2 c. chopped nuts, 1 1/2 c. semisweet chocolate chips and 1 tsp. vanilla. Stir until marshmallows melt. Pour into buttered 8" or 9" pan. Cool and cut into squares. Makes about 2 lbs.